Everyday
Healthy
COOKBOOK

Everyday Healthy

COOKBOOK

Recipes and a Meal Plan to Make Healthy Eating Easy

KATHY HODSON

Photographs by Laura Flippen

R

ROCKRIDGE
PRESS

For general information on our other products and services or to obtain technical support, please contact our Customer Care Department within the United States at (866) 744-2665, or outside the United States at (510) 253-0500.

Rockridge Press publishes its books in a variety of electronic and print formats. Some content that appears in print may not be available in electronic books, and vice versa.

TRADEMARKS: Rockridge Press and the Rockridge Press logo are trademarks or registered trademarks of Callisto Media Inc. and/or its affiliates, in the United States and other countries, and may not be used without written permission. All other trademarks are the property of their respective owners. Rockridge Press is not associated with any product or vendor mentioned in this book.

Interior and Cover Designer: Patricia Fabricant
Art Producer: Janice Ackerman
Editor: Cecily McAndrews
Production Editor: Ashley Polikoff

Photography & Food Styling: © 2020 Laura Flippen
Author Photo: © 2020 Joni Reed

ISBN: Print 978-1-64611-654-6 | eBook 978-1-64611-655-3

R0

For Joe, Jonah, and Caroline,
my favorite people to cook for.

Contents

Introduction

Back in my early twenties, my metabolism was so fast I could eat anything I wanted and not gain a pound. I was active and young and I honestly didn't think much about the food I was putting into my body.

Fast-forward to when I turned 30—everything changed. My metabolism slowed, I was now a mom to two kids, and I was in charge of making meals not only for myself but also for my whole family. I needed a plan to get myself back into a healthy groove.

When I started looking for ways to improve my family's meals, I was really confused. Some experts advised eliminating carbohydrates or red meat. Others said I should cut out dairy and legumes. There were so many programs and philosophies out there it made my head hurt.

I was not alone. The Centers for Disease Control stated that 9 out of 10 adults do not eat enough vegetables. The International Food Information Council says about one-third of Americans are dieting at any given point in time, and 80 percent of Americans are confused about what foods they should avoid and what foods they should eat.

Somewhere along the way, I realized I wasn't going to be able to stick with something long term that eliminated a whole food group. I needed to find a philosophy my family could adopt forever. That's when I realized eating healthy didn't require so many restrictions. I could enjoy my steak and potatoes with a side salad and not have to feel guilty about eating red meat. I could have a whole-wheat roll with my soup and not have to worry about carbs. Instead, the changes we made were incremental, achievable, and, most important, lasting. I'll tell you all about these changes in the pages that follow, but (spoiler alert) it involves more family meals, more whole grains, more produce, and far less guilt.

As I started sharing recipes that fit this philosophy on my blog, AMomsImpression.com, I realized how many people needed meals they could feel good about. I worked to create simple, realistic, delicious recipes with a short list of ingredients to help get dinner on the table quickly.

Eating healthy doesn't have to be complicated. It is easy to incorporate lighter meals into your current lifestyle in a way you can sustain and enjoy. I share recipes my family loves and will teach you how to meal plan to make it all easier to manage. All you need are some great-tasting natural ingredients and a few recipes to get you started.

CHAPTER ONE

Setting Yourself Up for Success

What does the word "healthy" mean to you?

Everyone has a different definition, but to me, eating healthy means giving my body the wholesome foods it needs so I feel good. The fact that you've picked up this book shows that you, too, are trying to create your own version of healthy.

I'm not a nutritionist or a doctor, but my recipes are road tested (by my kids, too!) and work in the real world. Throughout this book, I share my thoughts on health and how it affects the meals I make for my family.

My Healthy Eating Rules

Along my journey to healthy eating, I've come up with some guidelines for how to maintain a balance. I call them the Healthy Eating Rules, and all the recipes in this book reflect them.

1. **Focus on natural ingredients and limit processed foods**
    This is the number one rule of healthy eating. Whenever possible, go for fresh, natural ingredients. It isn't hard to make your own seasoned rice instead of reaching for a box mix. Your body digests unprocessed food more easily and you get more vitamins and nutrients, like fiber and complex carbohydrates, to fill you up with less food—and keep you fuller longer. Once you get used to this way of eating, it will become second nature.

2. **Plan your meals in advance so you aren't tempted to eat out**
    Meal planning not only saves time, it also keeps everyone on the same page so there's no discussion of pizza or takeout to tempt us off the plan. I share how I meal plan in chapter 2. This works for my husband, too, because he usually cooks once or twice a week. If he knows what's for dinner and that we have all the ingredients, he doesn't come home with burgers and fries that, although yummy, are not whole, healthy foods.

3. **Build good cooking and eating habits**
    Once you get into the habit of cooking every day, you will likely enjoy it more than you thought you would. I do most of the cooking in my house—not because my husband isn't willing or able, but because I love it. I find it therapeutic and relaxing.

4. **Get familiar with your spice drawer and fresh herbs**
    The biggest complaint I hear about eating healthy is that the food is bland. This is not true. Spices, whether fresh or dried, make everything flavorful and delicious. Learn which spices complement the foods you enjoy most, and use them liberally. See page 7 for a list of foods I suggest stocking in the refrigerator, freezer, and pantry.

5. **Have a little protein at every meal**
   Protein keeps hunger at bay and helps eliminate mindless snacking between meals. Consuming enough protein (animal- or plant-based) is essential to maintaining a healthy lifestyle.

6. **Remember that little changes add up**
   An adjustment doesn't have to be huge to be meaningful—in fact, the small ones can matter most. I now eat a salad for lunch at least three times a week, I replaced white bread with whole-wheat, and I eliminated cream from my morning coffee. I don't even think about these things anymore, but they have made a difference in my overall health.

7. **Introduce at least one new food a week**
   What's the worst that could happen? If someone's not a fan, you'll be having dinner again tomorrow.

8. **Stay hydrated**
   We all know how important it is to stay hydrated. Our body won't function to the best of its ability without enough water. Still, this rule is the hardest for me to follow. To help, I keep a pitcher of water in the refrigerator with some cucumber and lemon slices to flavor it.

9. **Treat yourself now and again**
   You have to be able to indulge every once in a while. The goal of healthy eating isn't to banish all cookies from your life forever, but to give your body the nutrients it needs to work properly and stay healthy. Healthy eating is about moderation. For example, I love salami, so sometimes I have a little processed food for a snack. Just not every day.

10. **Don't just enjoy your food; enjoy your meal**
    Some of my most cherished childhood memories took place at the dinner table, so we try to make mealtime an experience. We have a rule that electronic devices aren't allowed at the table. We talk about our day and have conversations as a family. When I introduce new recipes to the family, we talk about them and share our thoughts on what we like or dislike about the meal.

How to Use This Book

This book is meant to be a real-world guide to help you make healthier food choices. You will find resources, tips, and tricks I have learned along my journey to healthier eating, as well as 100 easy, delicious recipes you and your family will love. I hope this book will help you fit healthy meals into your current lifestyle.

THE TWO-WEEK MEAL PLAN

My life changed five years ago when I started meal planning. Since I started planning and preparing meals on Sundays, my family eats healthier and, as an added bonus, we spend less on food. Taking one day to plan makes me more efficient, and I spend a lot less time cooking during the week. It has been a game-changer for our busy family.

Chapter 2 shows you how to create a meal plan that works for your lifestyle. A typical meal plan will outline breakfast, lunch, and dinner for a week or two. To make shopping and food prep easy, the meals often share similar ingredients. A shopping list is included with the meal plans. You will also learn what to look for in recipes when you start creating your own meal plans.

THE RECIPES

The recipes in this book are easy to incorporate into your lifestyle. They are not complicated and do not use exotic ingredients. I cook everyday meals with ingredients I can easily find at my grocery store. I have included breakfast, lunch, and dinner recipes in every chapter so you have healthy options throughout the day.

Look through the chapters to find a recipe that fits your schedule. If you need a quick meal, check out the 30-minute recipes in chapter 4. If you don't want to stand over a hot stove, chapter 3 has some great suggestions for no-cook meals. If you have more time to prep in the morning or need a quick dinner solution, check out the delicious slow cooker and electric pressure cooker meals in chapter 7.

Each recipe contains these helpful features:

- All recipes are easy to make, and require **no more than 30 minutes of prep time**. Some recipes do require additional time for chilling, resting, or marinating, but those times are indicated.

- Each recipe has a **manageable list of recognizable ingredients**. If I have suggestions for substitutions, you will find them here as well.

- I have learned a few things over the years, and I share my **helpful tips** along the way, including shortcuts.

- **Nutritional calculations** will help you find recipes that fit your dietary needs.

SPECIAL DIETS WELCOME

As a parent of a child with dietary allergies, I know how important it is to control what's in the meals I feed my family. Each recipe in this book is labeled with icons to identify any special diet categories. Look for the following icons under the recipe title:

GLUTEN-FREE   **KID FRIENDLY**   **VEGETARIAN**   **LOW CALORIE**

Take a quick look at a recipe's easy-to-read ingredients list to determine whether the meal is a good fit for your family. Over the years, I have gotten very good at finding substitutions for things my son is allergic to, so I also offer substitution ideas for ingredients you can modify to fit certain dietary restrictions.

Filling Your Refrigerator, Freezer, and Pantry

It's not enough to have a plan for what to eat; it is equally important to keep healthy ingredients in your kitchen.

SHOP SMARTER

There are a lot of choices available when shopping for healthy foods. In addition to the grocery store, I love taking my family to our farmers' market to pick up local produce. We often find honey and maple syrup there, too. Not only do we get fresh foods, we also support small farms in our area.

For specialty items, there are a few health-food stores near us. Although they can be more expensive than traditional supermarkets, I have found they are actually more economical for buying bulk foods like oats, whole-wheat flour, plant-based protein powder, and dried fruits and nuts.

Every other Sunday my daughter and I head to the grocery store with our shopping list to do a larger shopping trip where we stock up on basics for our menu plan. As a result, we have to make only a few smaller trips during the week to purchase perishable foods. This cuts back on food waste as well as total time spent at the store.

I recommend mapping your shopping list to your local supermarket. I start at the back of the store and work my way toward the cash registers. When I create my grocery list, I make sure the beverages are at the top because they are in the back of the store. I then list the items I need, aisle by aisle. This method doesn't take long and ensures I don't leave anything off my list. It is a huge time-saver.

ITEMS TO KEEP ON HAND

Make sure you keep your refrigerator, freezer, and pantry stocked with wholesome staples. These items are the basis for many recipes in this book, and they're the fundamentals you need to create your own healthy meals. These items may vary from family to family, but this is what works for us.

REFRIGERATOR

- Apples
- Avocados
- Carrots
- Cheese: Cheddar, part-skim mozzarella, Parmesan
- Cream cheese, low-fat
- Eggs, large
- Milk
- Spinach
- Yogurt, low-fat plain Greek

FREEZER

- Frozen fruit: bananas, blueberries, strawberries
- Frozen vegetables: broccoli, Brussels sprouts, corn, mixed stir-fry vegetables

PANTRY

- Bread: pita, naan, whole-wheat sandwich bread
- Canned goods: black beans, low-sodium; broth, low-sodium (chicken and vegetable); chickpeas, low-sodium; tomatoes
- Garlic
- Honey
- Maple syrup
- Oats: old-fashioned and steel-cut
- Oil, extra-virgin olive and sesame
- Onions
- Pasta: rigatoni, whole-wheat spaghetti
- Rice: brown, white
- Spices: chili powder, cinnamon, cumin, garlic powder, Italian seasoning, onion powder, oregano, paprika, pepper, red pepper flakes, salt
- Vinegar: apple cider, balsamic, red-wine

CONVENIENCE CAN BE HEALTHY

We can all use shortcuts in the kitchen, and the grocery store is full of fresh, healthy convenience items that can save you a lot of time. These are natural, fresh, whole foods that aren't processed beyond being peeled or sliced.

- **FROZEN FRUIT:** Hello, smoothies!

- **FROZEN HERBS AND GINGER:** Fresh herbs and aromatics make all the difference, but sometimes it's hard to use them all before they spoil. You can find cubes of herbs frozen with oil for cooking. I use cilantro and ginger in a lot of my recipes.

- **FROZEN STIR-FRY VEGGIES:** Frozen vegetables are picked at the peak of freshness and flash frozen to keep as much of their nutrients as possible. A bag of these vegetables, a protein, and some spices equals a quick meal.

- **MINCED GARLIC:** I am an advocate of using garlic in just about any dish. Having a jar of peeled, minced garlic saves a lot of time.

- **PREPPED RAW VEGETABLES AND BABY CARROTS:** I like to snack, and having cut vegetables available keeps me on track for healthy eating.

- **PRE-WASHED GREENS:** These are a staple in our refrigerator. We eat a lot of salads for lunches, so having a tub ready to go is a time-saver. We also love having fresh spinach for smoothies.

FLANK STEAK WITH CHIMICHURRI, PAGE 74

The Meal Plans

A meal plan is simply a list of what you're going to serve throughout the week. From the meal plan comes your shopping list, so you're prepped and ready to go for healthy meals all week long.

Meal planning is a great way to simplify your daily meal routine. Ideally, it will take the stress and guesswork out of figuring out what to cook for each meal, freeing up time and energy for other activities. You can expect fewer trips to the grocery store and less on-the-fly planning that can lead to unhealthy food choices. You can also save money by buying items for more than one meal and eating leftovers for lunch.

6 TIPS FOR SUCCESSFUL MEAL PLANNING

1. **Choose recipes for the week with similar ingredients.** Check the refrigerator to see what you need to use, then check the pantry to see what you have stocked. Plan recipes using those ingredients, if possible, so you can trim your grocery list a bit.

2. **Consider any events or obligations you have during the week, like basketball practice.** Those aren't the nights to try a new recipe. Instead, opt for leftovers or a quick one-skillet meal.

3. **Include some of your family's favorites.** Although it is nice to try new recipes, it is also important to satisfy your family's need for familiar foods.

4. **Take note of expiration dates on meats.** On your prep day, freeze anything you won't use until later in the week. Make a note about defrosting, and transfer the meat to the refrigerator the night before you plan to cook it.

5. **Keep a consistent schedule.** I like to plan our meals on Saturday and head to the grocery store on Sunday. I prep breakfasts and lunches for the week on Sunday afternoon and prep or make some vegetables and meats ahead of time.

6. **Plan for leftovers.** Doubling a recipe is a great way to have lunches for the next day (see chapter 7). Be sure to build them into your weekly menu plan.

To help get you started, here are two meal plans that provide options for breakfast, lunch, and dinner for the week and give you a variety of dishes to enjoy. Following each weekly meal plan is a shopping list you can copy and bring to the grocery store. Be sure to check your refrigerator and pantry before shopping to see what you might already have on hand. After you do your big shopping trip, wash the fruits and vegetables and do any prep listed to set you up for the week.

If you want to print out these meal plans and shopping lists, or use a blank one in the weeks going forward, head to callistomediabooks /EverydayHealthy.com.

DON'T FORGET SNACKS

Here are some simple, portable snack ideas to power you through hungry moments and keep you away from the chips or vending machine. Some can be made ahead, and all are simple and satisfying.

- **APPLE SLICES WITH ALMOND BUTTER:** Use any type of nut butter. We like Honeycrisp and Gala apples for snacking.

- **AVOCADO TOAST:** You can make avocado toast a billion different ways. Smash up your avocado with a fork, spread it on some toasted bread, and add toppings. I like mine with tomato slices.

- **HARD-BOILED EGGS WITH EVERYTHING BAGEL SEASONING:** I hard-boil 6 to 10 eggs on Sunday when I meal prep. They will keep, refrigerated with their shells on, for up to 1 week.

- **BANANA SUSHI:** Spread some chocolate-hazelnut spread on a tortilla and roll it up around a peeled banana. Slice and snack.

- **TRAIL MIX:** My family loves mixing up our own trail mix and snacking on it throughout the week. Bonus: It's great for lunch boxes, too. We mix together peanuts, pretzels, dried fruit, chocolate chunks, and dried banana chips. Store in an airtight container.

RICE IS NICE

Some nights, having an extra pot boiling is too much to handle, which is why I find it useful to cook some of my side dishes ahead of time, especially rice and quinoa. They're nutritious, perfect for fast and easy meals, and will last up to 6 days in an airtight container in the refrigerator or 6 months in the freezer. When I do my prep on Sunday afternoon, I usually start with about 2 cups uncooked rice (either white or brown) to make 6 cups cooked rice for the week.

These recipes use cooked rice or quinoa:

- Quinoa-Zucchini Taco Bowls (page 60)
- Sweet & Spicy Soy-Glazed Tofu (page 61)
- Use-It-All-Up Leftover Fried Rice (page 62)
- Greek Chicken & Rice Bowl (page 65)
- Easy Coconut Curry Shrimp (page 88)
- Vegetarian Stuffed Peppers (page 134)
- Cashew Chicken (page 137)
- Easy Beef & Broccoli (page 140)
- Slow Cooker Pork Carnitas (page 148)

BROCCOLI EGG BITES (MINI-OMELETS), PAGE 128

Week 1 Meal Plan

SUNDAY

BREAKFAST	Easy Potato Breakfast Hash (page 78)
LUNCH	Wild Rice Soup (page 83)
DINNER	Sheet Pan Chicken Fajitas (page 112; leftovers reserved for Easy Chicken Fajita Salad)
PREP	DOUBLE BATCH: Breakfast Egg Muffins (page 52; 12 muffins)
	DOUBLE BATCH: Protein-Packed No-Bake Breakfast Bars (page 28)
	Freeze banana slices and strawberries for Peanut Butter & Jelly Smoothie (page 31) and Pineapple & Mango Smoothie Bowl (page 32)

MONDAY

BREAKFAST	LEFTOVER: Breakfast Egg Muffins
LUNCH	Easy Chicken Fajita Salad (page 113; made with leftovers from Sheet Pan Chicken Fajitas, page 112)
DINNER	Egg Roll in a Bowl (page 95)

TUESDAY

BREAKFAST	LEFTOVER: Protein-Packed No-Bake Breakfast Bars
LUNCH	LEFTOVER: Wild Rice Soup
DINNER	Smoked Salmon & Asparagus Fettuccine (page 87)
PREP	Cook eggs for Thursday's egg salad

WEDNESDAY

BREAKFAST	LEFTOVER: Breakfast Egg Muffins
LUNCH	LEFTOVER: Easy Chicken Fajita Salad
DINNER	Sweet Potato & Black Bean Chili (page 85)
PREP	Make Egg Salad (page 45) for lunch tomorrow and Friday

THURSDAY

BREAKFAST	LEFTOVER: Protein-Packed No-Bake Breakfast Bars
LUNCH	Curried Egg Salad Sandwiches with Watercress (page 45)
DINNER	Chicken Pad Thai with Zoodles (page 91)

FRIDAY

BREAKFAST	Peanut Butter & Jelly Smoothie (page 31)
LUNCH	LEFTOVER: Curried Egg Salad Sandwiches with Watercress
DINNER	LEFTOVER: Sweet Potato & Black Bean Chili

SATURDAY

BREAKFAST	Pineapple & Mango Smoothie Bowl (page 32)
LUNCH	Everything-Seasoned Avocado Toast with Egg (page 53)
DINNER	Seared Steak with Garlic Mushrooms & Sautéed Spinach (page 73)

WEEK 1 SHOPPING LIST

CANNED AND BOTTLED

- Beans, black, low-sodium, 1 (15-ounce) can)
- Broth, low-sodium vegetable or chicken (2½ quarts)
- Pad Thai sauce, 1 (8-ounce) jar
- Salsa, 1 (16-ounce) jar
- Tomato sauce, 1 (8-ounce) can

DAIRY AND EGGS

- Butter (1 stick)
- Cheese, shredded, low-fat Cheddar (1 cup)
- Cheese, shredded, type of choice (2 cups)
- Eggs, large (2½ dozen)
- Milk, whole (1 quart)
- Yogurt, low-fat plain Greek (2 cups)

FROZEN FOODS

- Corn (1 cup)
- Mango chunks (3 cups)
- Pineapple chunks (1 cup)
- Strawberries (2½ cups)

MEAT

- Beef, sirloin steaks, 4 (1-inch-thick)
- Chicken, boneless, skinless breasts (3½ pounds)
- Ham, cooked, diced (⅔ cup; optional)
- Salmon, smoked (8 ounces)
- Turkey, ground or pork, ground (1½ pounds)

PANTRY

- Almonds, slivered (¼ cup)
- Coconut flakes, unsweetened (¼ cup)
- Everything bagel seasoning
- Fajita seasoning (½ cup or 2 [1.12-ounce] packets)
- Fettuccine, dried (8 ounces)
- Flaxseed, ground (6 tablespoons)
- Honey (1 cup)
- Oats, old-fashioned (2 cups)

- Oil, sesame
- Peanut butter (2 cups)
- Peanuts (¼ cup; optional)
- Raisins or chocolate chips (1 cup)
- Wild rice (1½ cups)

PRODUCE

- Asparagus (1 bunch)
- Avocados (3)
- Bananas (6)
- Bean sprouts (3½ ounces)
- Bell peppers, red (3), plus any color (4)
- Blueberries (1 pint)
- Brussels sprouts (1 cup)
- Carrots (6)
- Celery stalks (4)
- Chives (1 bunch; optional)
- Cilantro (1 bunch)
- Coleslaw mix, 1 (1-pound) bag
- Garlic (3 heads)
- Kale (1 bunch)
- Limes (6)
- Microgreens (¼ cup; optional)
- Mushrooms, baby bella (1 pound)
- Mushrooms, button (8 ounces)
- Onions (7)
- Parsley (1 bunch; optional)
- Pineapple chunks (1 cup)
- Potatoes (1 pound)
- Romaine lettuce heart (1)
- Scallions (1 bunch)
- Spinach, baby (10 cups, about 20 ounces)
- Sweet potatoes (2)
- Thyme (1 bunch; optional)
- Tomatoes (2)
- Tomatoes, grape (1 pint)
- Watercress (1 bunch)
- Zucchini (6)

OTHER

- Bread, whole-grain (12 slices)
- Protein powder, plant-based vanilla (9 tablespoons)
- Tortilla chips (1 bag; optional)
- Tortillas, 8-inch flour

CHECK YOUR PANTRY FOR . . .

- Bay leaves, black pepper, capers, chili powder, curry powder, Dijon mustard, dried oregano, extra-virgin olive oil (1½ cups), ground cinnamon, ground cumin, ground ginger, low-sodium soy sauce, nonstick cooking spray, salt, vanilla extract

Week 2 Meal Plan

SUNDAY

BREAKFAST   Sun-dried Tomato & Kale Frittata (page 55)

LUNCH   Chicken Tortilla Soup (page 84)

DINNER   Broiled Flank Steaks with Brussels Sprouts & Sweet Potatoes
(page 122; reserve leftover steak and sweet potatoes for tomorrow's
Steak Buddha Bowl, page 125)

PREP   Cook 1½ pounds chicken and shred it for the week. You will need at
least 3 cups.

MONDAY

BREAKFAST   **LEFTOVER:** Sun-dried Tomato & Kale Frittata

LUNCH   Chicken Caesar Wraps (page 47)

DINNER   Steak Buddha Bowl (page 125), made with leftover steak from
Broiled Flank Steaks with Brussels Sprouts & Sweet Potatoes
(page 122)

TUESDAY

BREAKFAST   The Ultimate Green Smoothie (page 30)

LUNCH   **LEFTOVER:** Chicken Tortilla Soup

DINNER   Lemon Pepper Chicken with Broccoli (page 92)

PREP   Make the Apple Granola Oatmeal (page 141) for tomorrow
and Friday.

WEDNESDAY

BREAKFAST	Apple Granola Oatmeal (page 141)
LUNCH	LEFTOVER: Chicken Caesar Wraps
DINNER	Teriyaki Salmon with Green Beans (page 132)

THURSDAY

BREAKFAST	The Ultimate Green Smoothie (page 30)
LUNCH	LEFTOVER: Lemon Pepper Chicken with Broccoli
DINNER	Rigatoni with Tomatoes & Spinach (page 86)

FRIDAY

BREAKFAST	LEFTOVER: Apple Granola Oatmeal
LUNCH	LEFTOVER: Rigatoni with Tomatoes & Spinach
DINNER	Chicken Burrito Bowls (page 136)

SATURDAY

BREAKFAST	Sausage, Kale & Quinoa Breakfast Skillet (page 79)
LUNCH	Green Goddess Pita Sandwiches (page 43)
DINNER	Simple Beef Stir-Fry (page 75)

WEEK 2 SHOPPING LIST

CANNED AND BOTTLED

- Artichoke hearts,
  1 (14-ounce) can
- Beans, black, low-sodium,
  2 (15-ounce) cans
- Broth, low-sodium chicken
  (2½ quarts)
- Chickpeas, low-sodium,
  1 (15-ounce) can
- Salsa, 1 (16-ounce) jar
- Tomatoes, diced,
  2 (14.5-ounce) cans
- Tomatoes, oil-packed sun-dried
  (¼ cup)

DAIRY AND EGGS

- Cheese, grated Parmesan
  (1½ cups)
- Cheese, shredded, low-fat
  Cheddar (1 cup)
- Cheese, shredded, type of
  choice (1 cup; optional)
- Eggs, large (6)
- Milk, almond (1 quart)
- Yogurt, low-fat plain Greek
  (3 cups)

FROZEN FOODS

- Blueberries (1 cup)
- Corn (3 cups)
- Strawberries (1 cup)

MEAT

- Beef, flank steak, 3 (1-pound)
- Chicken, boneless, skinless
  breasts (3 pounds)
- Chicken, thinly sliced boneless,
  skinless breasts (1½ pounds)
- Salmon, skin-on fillets,
  4 (6-ounce)
- Sausage, fully cooked, chicken
  (1 pound)

PANTRY

- Anchovy paste, 1 (2-ounce) tube (optional)
- Applesauce, unsweetened (2 cups)
- Barley, pearl (1 cup)
- Dates, pitted dried (2)
- Hemp seeds (¼ cup; optional)
- Herbes de Provence
- Honey (¾ cup)
- Oats, steel-cut (1½ cups)
- Oil, sesame (¼ cup)
- Raisins (½ cup; optional)
- Rigatoni (16 ounces)
- Sesame seeds
- Taco seasoning, 2 (1-ounce) packets)
- Walnuts, chopped (optional)

PRODUCE

- Apples (2)
- Arugula (6 ounces [4 cups])
- Avocados (2)
- Bananas (2)
- Basil (1 small bunch; optional)
- Bell peppers, red (1) and yellow (2)
- Broccoli florets (3 cups)
- Brussels sprouts (7 ounces [2 cups])
- Cilantro (1 small bunch; optional)
- Cucumber (1)
- Garlic (2 heads)
- Green beans (1 pound or 1 [1-pound] bag, frozen microwaveable)
- Jalapeño pepper (1)
- Kale (3 [10-ounce] bags or 3 large bunches)
- Lemons (3)
- Lettuce, romaine (2 heads)
- Lime (1)
- Mushrooms, sliced (2.6 ounces [1 cup])
- Onions, red (1) and your choice (2)
- Oranges (3)
- Parsley (1 bunch)
- Spinach, baby (3 [10-ounce] bags [7 cups])
- Sugar snap peas (¾ pound)
- Sweet potatoes (5)
- Tomato (1)
- Tomatoes, cherry (1 pint)
- Zucchini (1)

- Apple cider (1 cup)
- Pita breads, 8-inch whole-wheat (2)
- Tortilla chips (1 bag)
- Tortillas, 8-inch flour (4)

CHECK YOUR PANTRY FOR . . .

- Black pepper, brown rice (1 cup), cornstarch, dried basil, extra-virgin olive oil (2 cups), ground cinnamon, lemon pepper, low-sodium soy sauce, quinoa (1 cup), rice vinegar, salt, spicy brown mustard, Worcestershire sauce

OPEN-FACED PEACH & PROSCIUTTO SANDWICHES, PAGE 44

CHAPTER THREE

No-Cook Meals

Protein-Packed
No-Bake Breakfast Bars

MAKES 9 BARS • PREP TIME: 15 MINUTES, PLUS 1 HOUR CHILLING

I make a large batch of these breakfast bars at least once a month on my meal-prep Sunday. They freeze well. The kids love them in their lunch boxes with a little yogurt and fruit, or for breakfast with a smoothie. Flaxseed is a great source of fiber, antioxidants, and omega-3 essential fatty acids. You can find flaxseed already ground in the baking aisle. Because you can make these bars ahead, they are perfect for quick meals and grab-and-go breakfasts or snacks.

1 ripe banana

¾ cup peanut butter

¼ cup honey

1 teaspoon vanilla extract

1 cup old-fashioned oats

3 tablespoons ground flaxseed

3 tablespoons plant-based vanilla protein powder

1 teaspoon ground cinnamon

½ cup raisins or chocolate chips

1. In a large bowl, mash the banana with a fork. Stir in the peanut butter, honey, and vanilla until well combined.

2. In a medium bowl, stir together the oats, flaxseed, protein powder, and cinnamon. A bit at a time, pour the dry ingredients into the banana mixture and stir to blend, stopping to scrape the sides of the bowl as needed.

3. Fold in the raisins. Pour the mixture into an 8-by-8-inch baking pan and press it into an even layer. Cover the pan with plastic wrap and refrigerate for 1 hour.

4. Cut into 9 bars. Keep refrigerated in an airtight container for up to 1 week.

VARIATION TIP: Switch up the raisins for other types of dried fruit. You could also add nuts or coconut for a flavor twist.

PER SERVING (1 BAR): CALORIES: 249; FAT: 13G; SATURATED FAT: 2G; CHOLESTEROL: 0MG; CARBOHYDRATES: 28G; FIBER: 4G; PROTEIN: 10G; SODIUM: 100MG

Yogurt Crunch Bowl with Basil & Balsamic Strawberries

SERVES 4 • PREP TIME: 10 MINUTES, PLUS 20 MINUTES MARINATING

It isn't hard to elevate familiar foods to make them more interesting. Adding herbs to a familiar dish can change it into something completely new. I have been eating strawberry yogurt bowls for a long time, but adding a little basil and balsamic vinegar has turned this everyday dish into something special and delicious.

2 cups fresh strawberries, hulled and quartered

2 tablespoons honey

1 teaspoon balsamic vinegar

½ teaspoon dried basil

4 cups low-fat vanilla Greek yogurt

¼ cup granola

¼ cup slivered almonds (optional)

5 fresh basil leaves, stacked, rolled, and cut crosswise into thin strips (called chiffonade)

1. In a medium bowl, gently stir together the strawberries, honey, vinegar, and basil. Cover the bowl with plastic wrap and refrigerate for at least 20 minutes, or up to overnight.

2. Divide the yogurt into 4 serving bowls.

3. Top the yogurt with the strawberry mixture, granola, and almonds (if using).

4. Garnish with the basil chiffonade.

LOVE YOUR LEFTOVERS: Double the macerated strawberries in step 1 and keep them refrigerated, covered, for up to 3 days. Use the berries in a smoothie the next morning or serve over vanilla frozen yogurt for dessert.

PER SERVING: CALORIES: 315; FAT: 4G; SATURATED FAT: 2G; CHOLESTEROL: 27MG; CARBOHYDRATES: 53G; FIBER: 2G; PROTEIN: 18G; SODIUM: 121MG

The Ultimate Green Smoothie

SERVES 2 • PREP TIME: 5 MINUTES

It is important to incorporate dark, leafy greens into your diet whenever and wherever you can because they're full of vitamins and antioxidants that are good for your body. I like to add hemp seeds to my green smoothie, too: They contain omega-9 fatty acids, calcium, iron, magnesium, and zinc and are beneficial for your overall health. If you prefer, substitute chia seeds or plant-based protein powder for the hemp seeds.

1 cup water or freshly squeezed orange juice, plus more as needed

1 cup fresh baby spinach

1 cup chopped kale

½ cup frozen blueberries

½ cup frozen strawberries

½ cup low-fat plain Greek yogurt

1 banana, sliced and frozen

1 pitted date

2 tablespoons hemp seeds (optional)

In a blender, combine the water, spinach, kale, blueberries, strawberries, yogurt, banana, date, and hemp seeds (if using). Blend on high speed until smooth. If the smoothie is too thick or too difficult to blend, add more water until it is the right consistency. If your berries are fresh instead of frozen, add a few ice cubes.

INGREDIENT TIP: Look for frozen fruit in various combinations, such as strawberries and blueberries in one bag, to save on grocery costs, or buy fresh fruit on sale and freeze it yourself.

VARIATION TIP: To make this smoothie kid friendly, double the amount of spinach and omit the kale. Fruit can mask the flavor of spinach more easily than that of kale. If you don't have a date, use 1 tablespoon honey.

PER SERVING: CALORIES: 165; FAT: 2G; SATURATED FAT: 1G; CHOLESTEROL: 8MG; CARBOHYDRATES: 32G; FIBER: 6G; PROTEIN: 8G; SODIUM: 69MG

Peanut Butter & Jelly Smoothie

SERVES 2 • PREP TIME: 10 MINUTES

All the flavors of a classic peanut butter and jelly sandwich in a glass. I make this smoothie for my kids before they head off to school. They love it, especially with a bowl of strawberries alongside. For an indulgence, throw in a few mini chocolate chips, too.

2 cups milk (dairy or nondairy), plus more as needed

2½ cups frozen strawberries

2 bananas, cut into chunks and frozen

¼ cup peanut butter

3 tablespoons plant-based vanilla protein powder

1 tablespoon honey

In a blender, combine the milk, strawberries, bananas, peanut butter, protein powder, and honey. Blend on high speed until you get a drinkable consistency, for about 1 minute. If the mixture is too thick, add more milk.

COOKING TIP: When I have a bunch of overripe bananas, I slice and freeze them on a parchment-lined baking sheet. When they are completely frozen, I transfer them to freezer bags, about 16 slices (2 bananas) in each. Doing so makes it simple to grab a bag and throw it in the blender for a smoothie.

PER SERVING: CALORIES: 542; FAT: 20G; SATURATED FAT: 5G; CHOLESTEROL: 15MG; CARBOHYDRATES: 71G; FIBER: 9G; PROTEIN: 28G; SODIUM: 274MG

Pineapple & Mango Smoothie Bowl

SERVES 2 • PREP TIME: 10 MINUTES

Smoothie bowls are extremely popular at the moment, and for good reason: They are filled with delicious fruit and are a good source of healthy carbohydrates, making them ideal for an easy breakfast or lunch before a workout. These bowls are thicker than a traditional smoothie, so eat with a spoon. Once you get the method down, you can create any type of smoothie bowl you can dream up.

FOR THE BASE

1 cup milk (dairy or nondairy), plus more as needed

3 cups frozen mango chunks

1 cup frozen pineapple chunks

¾ cup frozen banana chunks

FOR THE BOWLS

1 cup fresh pineapple chunks

½ cup fresh blueberries

1 banana, sliced

¼ cup unsweetened coconut flakes

¼ cup slivered almonds

TO MAKE THE BASE

In a blender, combine the milk, mango, pineapple, and banana. Blend on high speed for about 1 minute until you get a thick consistency. If this mixture is too thick, add more milk. Pour into 2 shallow bowls.

TO MAKE THE BOWLS

Top each smoothie base with half each of the pineapple, blueberries, banana, coconut, and almonds.

INGREDIENT TIP: Look for frozen fruit in various combinations, such as a tropical fruit blend in one bag, to save on grocery costs. An alternative is to purchase fresh fruit on sale and freeze it yourself. Cut the fruit into 1-inch chunks and freeze on a parchment-lined baking sheet. When the fruit has frozen, store in quart-size freezer bags.

VARIATION TIP: If you are not a fan of tropical flavors like mango, use your favorite fruits, like strawberries. My kids love a few mini marshmallows as a topping for a little extra treat.

PER SERVING: CALORIES: 516; FAT: 14G; SATURATED FAT: 6G; CHOLESTEROL: 8MG; CARBOHYDRATES: 93G; FIBER: 12G; PROTEIN: 11G; SODIUM: 67MG

Easy Gazpacho with Shrimp

SERVES 4 TO 6 • PREP TIME: 30 MINUTES, PLUS 30 MINUTES CHILLING TIME

Gazpacho is very popular in Spain and many other places. I love that I can enjoy this soup without having to turn on the stove. This chilled soup is also a great option to pack for your lunch—no reheating required.

6 large plum tomatoes, halved, seeded, and diced, divided

1 large cucumber, peeled, seeded, and diced (about 2 cups), divided

1 cup diced red onion, divided

1 green bell pepper, diced, divided

2 garlic cloves, minced

2 cups low-sodium tomato juice

¼ cup extra-virgin olive oil

2 tablespoons red-wine vinegar

1 teaspoon hot sauce

½ teaspoon salt

½ teaspoon freshly ground black pepper

8 jumbo shrimp, cooked

1. In a blender, combine 3 tomatoes, half the cucumber, half the red onion, half the bell pepper, the garlic, and the tomato juice. Blend until smooth. Transfer to a medium bowl.

2. Stir in the olive oil, vinegar, hot sauce, salt, and black pepper. Cover the bowl with plastic wrap and refrigerate for 30 minutes.

3. When ready to serve, fold in the remaining tomatoes, cucumber, red onion, and bell pepper. Pour the soup into bowls and garnish with the cooked shrimp. Refrigerate any remaining soup in an airtight container for up to 5 days.

VARIATION TIP: For a vegan meal, omit the shrimp. My husband loves using spicy tomato juice, which adds a little kick to the soup.

PER SERVING: CALORIES: 224; FAT: 14G; SATURATED FAT: 2G; CHOLESTEROL: 43MG; CARBOHYDRATES: 17G; FIBER: 4G; PROTEIN: 8G; SODIUM: 456MG

DRESSING FOR THE OCCASION

I always have a jar or two of homemade salad dressing knocking around my refrigerator. It takes only a minute to throw together, is free of any weird ingredients you might find in store-bought options, and makes a lunchtime salad so much more appealing. Here are a few of my favorites. You'll find them in recipes throughout the book.

Each recipe makes enough dressing for a meal-size salad serving 4 to 6 people (about 2 tablespoons dressing per serving). If you want extra dressing for additional salads through the week, double the ingredients.

Maple Mustard Vinaigrette MAKES ABOUT ¾ CUP

¼ cup apple cider or balsamic vinegar

1½ tablespoons maple syrup

2 teaspoons spicy brown mustard

½ teaspoon salt

½ teaspoon freshly ground black pepper

½ cup extra-virgin olive oil

In a jar, whisk the vinegar, maple syrup, mustard, salt, and pepper to combine. Slowly drizzle in the olive oil, whisking constantly. Use immediately or cover and store for up to 1 week. Shake the jar or whisk the dressing before using.

PER 2-TABLESPOON SERVING: CALORIES: 175; FAT: 18G; SATURATED FAT: 3G; CHOLESTEROL: 0MG; CARBOHYDRATES: 4G; FIBER: <1G; PROTEIN: 0G; SODIUM: 221MG

Zesty Lime Dressing MAKES ABOUT ¾ CUP

Zest of 1 lime

¼ cup freshly squeezed lime juice (about 3 limes)

2 garlic cloves, minced

1 teaspoon dried oregano

½ teaspoon ground cumin

⅓ cup extra-virgin olive oil

In a jar, whisk the lime zest, lime juice, garlic, oregano, and cumin to combine. Slowly drizzle in the olive oil, whisking constantly. Use immediately or cover and store for up to 1 week. Shake the jar or whisk the dressing before using.

PER 2-TABLESPOON SERVING: CALORIES: 112; FAT: 12G; SATURATED FAT: 2G; CHOLESTEROL: 0MG; CARBOHYDRATES: <1G; FIBER: <1G; PROTEIN: <1G; SODIUM: 1MG

Italian Dressing MAKES ABOUT 1 CUP

⅓ cup red-wine vinegar

2 teaspoons dried basil

1 tablespoon
    Italian seasoning

1 teaspoon salt

½ teaspoon
    garlic powder

½ cup extra-virgin
    olive oil

In a jar, whisk the vinegar, basil, Italian seasoning, salt, and garlic powder to combine. Slowly drizzle in the olive oil, whisking constantly. Use immediately or cover and store for up to a week. Shake the jar or whisk the dressing before using.

PER 2-TABLESPOON SERVING: CALORIES: 123; FAT: 14G; SATURATED FAT: 2G; CHOLESTEROL: 0MG; CARBOHYDRATES: <1G; FIBER: <1G; PROTEIN: <1; SODIUM: 291MG

Lighter Caesar Dressing MAKES 2 CUPS

1 cup low-fat plain
    Greek yogurt

¼ cup grated
    Parmesan cheese

2 tablespoons
    freshly squeezed
    lemon juice

1 tablespoon
    Dijon mustard

1 tablespoon
    Worcestershire
    sauce

1 tablespoon extra-
    virgin olive oil

2 teaspoons anchovy
    paste (optional)

2 garlic cloves, minced

½ teaspoon salt

¼ teaspoon
    freshly ground
    black pepper

In a large jar, whisk the yogurt, cheese, lemon juice, mustard, Worcestershire sauce, olive oil, anchovy paste (if using), garlic, salt, and pepper to combine. Use immediately or cover and store for up to 1 week. Shake the jar or whisk the dressing before using.

PER 2-TABLESPOON SERVING: CALORIES: 29; FAT: 2G; SATURATED FAT: <1G; CHOLESTEROL: 4MG; CARBOHYDRATES: 2G; FIBER: 0G; PROTEIN: 2G; SODIUM: 145MG

Tomato, Chickpea & Mozzarella Salad

SERVES 4 • PREP TIME: 10 MINUTES

This recipe is perfect for a lunch box because it is full of wholesome ingredients that will keep you full all day long, including plenty of protein and fiber.

1 (15-ounce) can low-sodium chickpeas, rinsed and drained

1 cup cherry tomatoes, halved

1 cucumber, chopped

1 red bell pepper, chopped

½ red onion, thinly sliced

½ cup mozzarella pearls

¼ cup fresh parsley, chopped

½ cup Italian Dressing (page 35)

1 avocado, pitted, peeled, and diced

1. In a large bowl, stir together the chickpeas, cherry tomatoes, cucumber, bell pepper, onion, mozzarella, and parsley.

2. Pour the dressing over the salad, and toss to coat. Stir in the avocado just before serving (if you're planning to save leftovers for later, add avocado only to the portion you're serving immediately).

3. Refrigerate leftovers in a covered container for up to 3 days.

VARIATION TIP: You could easily switch up the flavors in this salad for a Greek version: Swap feta cheese for the mozzarella and add 1 teaspoon dried oregano. Use fresh cilantro instead of parsley, if you prefer.

PER SERVING: CALORIES: 367; FAT: 24G; SATURATED FAT: 5G; CHOLESTEROL: 10MG; CARBOHYDRATES: 31G; FIBER: 11G; PROTEIN: 10G; SODIUM: 325MG

Arugula Salad with Berries & Maple-Poppy Seed Dressing

SERVES 4 • PREP TIME: 10 MINUTES

This light salad is perfect for a summer picnic. The little bit of sweetness from the maple syrup in the dressing pairs so well with the berries. Try other seasonal fruits throughout the year.

4 cups arugula

1¼ cups halved fresh
  strawberries

1 cup blueberries

¾ cup whole pecans

1½ tablespoons
  poppy seeds

½ cup Maple Mustard
  Vinaigrette (page 34–
  I like it with balsamic
  vinegar for this salad)

1. In a large bowl, combine the arugula, strawberries, blueberries, and pecans.

2. In a small bowl, whisk the poppy seeds and vinaigrette to combine. Pour the dressing over the salad and toss to coat.

VARIATION TIP: Arugula can be a little spicy for some people. Use baby spinach, if preferred, or even a 50-50 blend of spinach and arugula to suit your tastes. If I have the time, I also love toasting the pecans in a 350°F oven for 8 to 10 minutes, stirring once or twice; doing so deepens the flavor.

PER SERVING: CALORIES: 372; FAT: 34G; SATURATED FAT: 4G; CHOLESTEROL: 0MG; CARBOHYDRATES: 16G; FIBER: 5G; PROTEIN: 4G; SODIUM: 230MG

Apple Orchard Spinach & Feta Salad

SERVES 4 • PREP TIME: 15 MINUTES

In fall, my family always goes apple picking. My kids adore filling their wagon with all types of apples, but Honeycrisp is their favorite. We end up with an abundance of apples, so I love finding new recipes for them. You can use any type of apple you love.

4 cups fresh baby spinach

2 medium Honeycrisp apples, thinly sliced

1 cup chopped walnuts

½ cup dried sweetened cranberries

½ cup crumbled feta cheese

½ cup Maple Mustard Vinaigrette (page 34)

1. In a large bowl, combine the spinach, apples, walnuts, and cranberries. Fold in the feta cheese.

2. Pour the vinaigrette over the salad and toss to coat.

SUBSTITUTION TIP: If you have a nut allergy, use sunflower seeds instead of walnuts.

PER SERVING: CALORIES: 512; FAT: 42G; SATURATED FAT: 7G; CHOLESTEROL: 17MG; CARBOHYDRATES: 32G; FIBER: 6G; PROTEIN: 8G; SODIUM: 466MG

Southwestern Tuna & Three-Bean Salad

SERVES 6 • PREP TIME: 20 MINUTES

Tuna is a great low-calorie, high-protein food that really fills you up. I used to smother it in mayonnaise and relish for a sandwich, but there are so many healthier ways to eat tuna. When I think I don't have anything to make for lunch or dinner, I head to my pantry and pull together this recipe. Beans are a great source of fiber and vitamin B and can help lower cholesterol.

1 (15-ounce) can low-sodium black beans, rinsed and drained

1 (15-ounce) can low-sodium great northern beans, rinsed and drained

1 (15-ounce) can low-sodium dark red kidney beans, rinsed and drained

1 (15-ounce) can whole kernel corn, drained

2 (5-ounce) cans chunk light tuna, drained

½ cup halved grape tomatoes

½ cup diced red onion

½ cup fresh cilantro leaves, finely chopped

¾ cup Zesty Lime Dressing (page 34)

1. In a large bowl, stir together the black beans, great northern beans, kidney beans, corn, tuna, tomatoes, and onion. Fold in the cilantro.

2. Pour the dressing over the salad and toss to coat.

3. Refrigerate leftovers in an airtight container for up to 3 days.

VARIATION TIP: To make a creamier dressing, add 2 table-spoons low-fat plain Greek yogurt to the dressing before mixing with the salad. The yogurt goes really well with the beans and is a healthier option than mayonnaise.

PER SERVING: CALORIES: 386; FAT: 15G; SATURATED FAT: 2G; CHOLESTEROL: 17MG; CARBOHYDRATES: 45G; FIBER: 14G; PROTEIN: 21G; SODIUM: 441MG

Chicken, Pear, Walnut & Gorgonzola Salad

SERVES 4 • PREP TIME: 15 MINUTES

If you love the tang of Gorgonzola cheese, you are going to love this combination. The pear and raisins add a sweetness to the dish that complements the cheese, and the walnuts provide a nice crunch. This salad is perfect for any season and can be served as a side or main course. Making this dish vegetarian is as simple as removing the chicken. It tastes great either way.

4 cups chopped romaine lettuce

1 cup shredded cooked chicken

1 pear, thinly sliced

½ cup Gorgonzola cheese

½ cup chopped walnuts

¼ cup raisins (optional)

½ cup Maple Mustard Vinaigrette (page 34)

1. Place the lettuce in a large serving bowl. Add the chicken, pear, Gorgonzola cheese, walnuts, and raisins (if using). Toss to combine.

2. Pour the vinaigrette over the salad and toss to coat.

INGREDIENT TIP: The general rule for a main-dish salad is to have at least 1 cup romaine lettuce per person. If you are going to serve this salad as a side dish, reduce the amount of lettuce to ½ cup per person.

PER SERVING: CALORIES: 408; FAT: 33G; SATURATED FAT: 6G; CHOLESTEROL: 42MG; CARBOHYDRATES: 12G; FIBER: 3G; PROTEIN: 18G; SODIUM: 382MG

Kitchen Sink Italian Salad

SERVES 6 • PREP TIME: 20 MINUTES

Remember in chapter 1 when we talked about treating yourself occasionally? I treat myself with pepperoni. For a leaner alternative, this recipe uses turkey pepperoni, but you can use whatever you like. This is a great recipe when you crave Italian food but want something light as well.

½ red onion, thinly sliced

1 small romaine lettuce heart, chopped (about 6 cups)

1 small head radicchio, chopped

1 (8-ounce) package turkey pepperoni, chopped

1 cucumber, chopped

1 cup halved cherry tomatoes

1 red bell pepper, cut into strips

½ cup banana pepper rings

2 tablespoons shredded Parmesan cheese (optional)

1 teaspoon freshly ground black pepper

¾ cup Italian Dressing (page 35)

1. Place the red onion slices in a small bowl of ice water and soak for at least 10 minutes. Doing so helps mellow the flavor.

2. In a large bowl, combine the romaine lettuce, radicchio, pepperoni, cucumber, tomatoes, bell pepper, banana pepper, and Parmesan cheese (if using).

3. Drain the onion slices, pat dry with a towel, and fold them into the salad. Season with the black pepper.

4. Pour the dressing over the portion of the salad you're planning to serve immediately and toss to coat.

5. Undressed leftover salad can be kept covered with plastic wrap for up to 2 days.

SUBSTITUTION TIP: Substitute diced cooked chicken breast for the pepperoni for a healthier alternative. If you don't have any dried basil for the dressing, use Italian seasoning instead, or substitute ½ cup fresh basil.

PER SERVING: CALORIES: 203; FAT: 17G; SATURATED FAT: 3G; CHOLESTEROL: 17MG; CARBOHYDRATES: 8G; FIBER: 3G; PROTEIN: 8G; SODIUM: 658MG

Cucumber & Avocado Sandwich

SERVES 4 • PREP TIME: 10 MINUTES

I love cucumbers. When you mix them with avocado you get a creamy, crunchy combination that still feels light–perfect for a light lunch or dinner. I like to pair this sandwich with fruit for a full meal. For a little extra texture and crunch, toast the bread.

Juice of 1 lemon

1 avocado, peeled, pitted, and thinly sliced

½ cup whipped vegetable cream cheese (4 ounces)

8 whole-wheat bread slices

1 cup alfalfa sprouts

1 English cucumber, thinly sliced

¼ teaspoon salt

¼ teaspoon freshly ground black pepper

1. Drizzle the lemon juice over the avocado slices and set aside.

2. Spread the cream cheese on the bread.

3. Evenly divide and layer the alfalfa sprouts and cucumber among 4 slices of bread. Season with the salt and pepper.

4. Layer the avocado slices on top of the cucumbers and top with the 4 remaining bread slices. Serve immediately.

SUBSTITUTION TIP: This sandwich can easily be made vegan by replacing the cream cheese with hummus. If you don't have cream cheese on hand, try goat cheese.

PER SERVING: CALORIES: 349; FAT: 15G; SATURATED FAT: 4G; CHOLESTEROL: 15MG; CARBOHYDRATES: 52G; FIBER: 14G; PROTEIN: 13G; SODIUM: 569MG

Green Goddess Pita Sandwiches

SERVES 2 • PREP TIME: 20 MINUTES

I have made 101 different versions of chicken salad sandwiches, but recently, when looking for an alternative, I realized chickpeas were the perfect substitute for chicken. These green goddess pitas are filled with fresh vegetables. For some crunch, add a diced apple or some sunflower seeds.

1 avocado, halved and pitted

1 cup canned low-sodium chickpeas, rinsed and drained

½ cup thinly sliced red onion

1 jalapeño pepper, seeded and finely diced (optional)

Juice of 1 lime

1 teaspoon spicy brown mustard

¼ teaspoon salt

¼ teaspoon freshly ground black pepper

2 (8-inch) whole-wheat pita breads, halved

1 cup fresh baby spinach

1. Scoop the avocado flesh into a medium bowl. Add the chickpeas and mash together using a fork.
2. Stir in the onion, jalapeño (if using), lime juice, mustard, salt, and pepper.
3. Stuff the pita halves with the spinach.
4. Spoon the chickpea mixture into the pita halves and serve immediately.

INGREDIENT TIP: Did you know avocados have more potassium than bananas? Avocados are full of fiber and heart-healthy monounsaturated fatty acids, so they bring not only a lot of flavor and creaminess to meals, but also a lot of health benefits, too.

PER SERVING: CALORIES: 498; FAT: 16G; SATURATED FAT: 2G; CHOLESTEROL: 0MG; CARBOHYDRATES: 76G; FIBER: 19G; PROTEIN: 16G; SODIUM: 765MG

Open-Faced Peach & Prosciutto Sandwiches

SERVES 4 • PREP TIME: 15 MINUTES

Cottage cheese is a great source of calcium and protein. I am not a big fan of eating a plain bowl of it, but paired with fruit, honey, and prosciutto, it becomes a recipe I put on repeat.

1 cup low-fat cottage cheese

Zest of 1 lemon

¼ teaspoon salt

¼ teaspoon freshly ground black pepper

4 whole-wheat bread slices, toasted

1 cup arugula (optional)

1 tablespoon honey

4 prosciutto slices

2 peaches, sliced

2 tablespoons chopped fresh mint

1. In a small bowl, stir together the cottage cheese, lemon zest, salt, and pepper to combine.

2. Divide the cottage cheese mixture among the 4 toast slices and spread it evenly.

3. Top each with ¼ cup arugula (if using).

4. Drizzle the honey on top.

5. Top each sandwich with prosciutto, peaches, and mint.

SUBSTITUTION TIP: If you don't enjoy mint, use fresh basil. If you don't have any cottage cheese, use ricotta. I enjoy the spicy flavor of arugula, but if you don't, use baby spinach or omit the greens; the sandwich will still taste delicious.

PER SERVING: CALORIES: 243; FAT: 7G; SATURATED FAT: 1G; CHOLESTEROL: 19MG; CARBOHYDRATES: 34G; FIBER: 6G; PROTEIN: 16G; SODIUM: 616MG

Curried Egg Salad Sandwiches with Watercress

SERVES 4 • PREP TIME: 30 MINUTES

I've been eating egg salad as long as I can remember. This is a great recipe to double up and enjoy throughout the week. This version is a little spicy, with the addition of the curry powder and watercress. Watercress is a bitter green and adds a nice little peppery flavor to the sandwiches, and it pairs well with the creamy egg salad.

6 large hard-boiled eggs, peeled and chopped

¼ cup diced celery

¼ cup low-fat plain Greek yogurt

1 tablespoon Dijon mustard

1¼ teaspoons curry powder

¼ teaspoon kosher salt

¼ teaspoon freshly ground black pepper

8 whole-grain bread slices

½ cup watercress, chopped

1. In a medium bowl, stir together the eggs, celery, yogurt, mustard, curry powder, salt, and pepper.

2. Toast the bread, if you like.

3. Divide the egg salad among 4 slices of bread and spread it into an even layer.

4. Top each with watercress and a second slice of bread.

COOKING TIP: I like to make a dozen hard-boiled eggs in my pressure cooker when I food prep on Sunday. Hard-boiled eggs can last up to 1 week in the refrigerator with their shells on. Label the container with the date so you remember to eat them in time.

PER SERVING: CALORIES: 327; FAT: 11G; SATURATED FAT: 3G; CHOLESTEROL: 281MG; CARBOHYDRATES: 44G; FIBER: 10G; PROTEIN: 21G; SODIUM: 679MG

Caprese Chicken Salad Wrap

SERVES 4 • PREP TIME: 20 MINUTES

This sandwich has so many flavors and textures: It's creamy, tangy, crunchy, and herbaceous from the homemade pesto. Store-bought pesto is just fine if you don't have the time to make your own.

4 (8-inch) flour tortillas (I use spinach tortillas) or flatbreads

½ cup Easy Pesto (page 58) or store-bought pesto

2 cups shredded cooked chicken

2 cups chopped romaine lettuce

2 small roma tomatoes, sliced

1 cup shredded, part-skim mozzarella cheese

¼ cup store-bought balsamic glaze

1. Place the tortillas on a flat work surface, such as a cutting board. Spread 2 tablespoons of pesto on each tortilla.

2. Divide the chicken among the tortillas and top each with the lettuce, tomatoes, and mozzarella cheese.

3. Drizzle the balsamic glaze on top.

4. Roll up the tortillas, tucking in the sides as you go, and cut in half to serve.

VARIATION TIP: If you are not a fan of pesto, smash a large avocado and use that instead.

PER SERVING: CALORIES: 475; FAT: 16G; SATURATED FAT: 6G; CHOLESTEROL: 77MG; CARBOHYDRATES: 48G; FIBER: 3G; PROTEIN: 36G; SODIUM: 561MG

Chicken Caesar Wraps

SERVES 4 • PREP TIME: 15 MINUTES

Caesar dressing is one of my favorites, and I could eat my Lighter Caesar Dressing (page 35) on salads for lunch every day. This wrap is the perfect showcase for it—crunchy, salty, and protein filled.

4 (8-inch) flour tortillas

2 cups chopped romaine lettuce

1½ cups shredded cooked chicken

1 yellow bell pepper, cut into strips

½ cup grated Parmesan cheese

½ cup Lighter Caesar Dressing (page 35)

1. Place the tortillas on a flat work surface, such as a cutting board. Divide the romaine lettuce among the tortillas, placing it in the middle of each.

2. Place the shredded chicken, bell pepper, and Parmesan cheese on top of the romaine.

3. Drizzle some dressing on top.

4. Roll up the tortillas, tucking in the sides as you go, and cut in half to serve.

VARIATION TIP: There are so many different tortilla flavor options. For this recipe, I love the sun-dried tomato or spinach variety. I add almonds or walnuts for extra crunch.

PER SERVING: CALORIES: 344; FAT: 11G; SATURATED FAT: 4G; CHOLESTEROL: 58MG; CARBOHYDRATES: 32G; FIBER: 3G; PROTEIN: 29G; SODIUM: 654MG

Roast Beef Lettuce Wraps

SERVES 4 • PREP TIME: 10 MINUTES

My family loves lettuce wraps. We like to wrap just about anything in lettuce, from tacos to chicken salad. The idea for roast beef wraps developed
when we ran out of bread and I was craving a roast beef sandwich. You can switch
these up a million different ways: Try adding cheese or substituting Easy Pesto
(page 58) for the mustard.

8 large butter lettuce or
romaine lettuce leaves

3 tablespoons Dijon
mustard or light
mayonnaise

12 roast beef slices

½ cucumber, diced

½ cup shredded carrots

¼ cup Italian Dressing
(page 35)

1 tablespoon chopped
fresh chives

1. Place the lettuce leaves on a flat work surface,
such as a cutting board. Spread each with
the mustard.

2. Divide the roast beef slices among the lettuce
leaves and top with the cucumber and carrots.

3. Drizzle with the Italian dressing. Sprinkle the
chives on top before rolling and serving.

INGREDIENT TIP: I prefer butter lettuce leaves because
they are thin and easy to work with. When I make these
wraps with butter lettuce, I usually serve two per person.
Romaine leaves do not fold or roll as easily, but they offer
a satisfying crunch.

PER SERVING: CALORIES: 154; FAT: 9G; SATURATED FAT: 2G;
CHOLESTEROL: 23MG; CARBOHYDRATES: 4G; FIBER: 1G;
PROTEIN: 12G; SODIUM: 592MG

Fresh Veggie Spring Rolls with Garlic-Chile Sauce

MAKES 8 ROLLS AND 1 CUP SAUCE • PREP TIME: 25 MINUTES

Spring rolls are one of my husband's favorite lunches, and some home-made Garlic-Chile Sauce (page 58) perks them right up. In a lunch box, they are a nice break from a sandwich or salad, and it's a fun way to eat a lot of vegetables.

8 rice paper wrappers

4 green lettuce leaves, halved lengthwise

1 cucumber, thinly sliced

1 red bell pepper, thinly sliced

1 avocado, pitted, peeled, and sliced

1 cup shredded carrots

1 cup chopped red cabbage

Garlic-Chile Sauce, store-bought or homemade (page 58), for dipping

Thai peanut sauce, for dipping (optional)

1. Fill a shallow dish with hot water that can fit your rice paper wrappers. One at a time, place a wrapper in the water for about 10 seconds, or until softened. Transfer the wrappers to a flat work surface, such as a cutting board.

2. Place a lettuce leaf half on top of a wrapper, then top with one-eighth each of the cucumber, bell pepper, avocado, carrots, and red cabbage. Fold in the sides. Roll up the wrapper tightly; it will seal itself. Repeat with the remaining wrappers and filling ingredients.

3. Serve with the Garlic-Chile Sauce and Thai peanut sauce (if using) for dipping.

COOKING TIP: If you find your rice paper wrappers are too thin or difficult to work with, double them, placing one on top of the other. (You'll need 16 rice paper wrappers for this.)

PER SERVING: CALORIES: 89; FAT: 4G; SATURATED FAT: 1G; CHOLESTEROL: 0MG; CARBOHYDRATES: 13G; FIBER: 3G; PROTEIN: 2G; SODIUM: 26MG

SIMPLE SHRIMP SCAMPI WITH ZUCCHINI, PAGE 63

CHAPTER FOUR

Lightning-Fast 30-Minute Meals

Breakfast Egg Muffins

MAKES 6 TO 8 MUFFINS • PREP TIME: 10 MINUTES • COOK TIME: 20 MINUTES

These egg muffins are not only delicious, but also healthy and perfect for meal planning. I usually double the batch and keep them in the freezer for quick and easy breakfasts—just put them in the refrigerator overnight to thaw so they are ready for the morning routine. I usually reheat them in the microwave. They are also very versatile, so use whatever ingredients you have in the refrigerator.

Nonstick cooking spray (optional)

6 large eggs

½ teaspoon salt

¼ teaspoon freshly ground black pepper

⅓ cup shredded low-fat Cheddar cheese

⅓ cup diced cooked ham (optional)

⅓ cup diced tomato

¼ cup fresh baby spinach, chopped

¼ cup diced onion

1. Preheat the oven to 375°F. Line 6 cups of a standard muffin tin with paper liners, or generously spray them with cooking spray.

2. In a medium bowl, whisk the eggs, salt, and pepper until smooth.

3. Stir in the Cheddar cheese, ham (if using), tomato, spinach, and onion. Divide the mixture among the prepared muffin cups, filling each about two-thirds full.

4. Bake for 16 to 19 minutes, or until a toothpick inserted into the middle of a muffin comes out clean. Let cool for a few minutes before removing the muffins from the tin.

5. Keep refrigerated in an airtight container for up to 5 days.

INGREDIENT TIP: Fresh spinach leaves can be a little difficult to work with if they are big. If yours are on the larger side, cut off the stems and place a few leaves at the bottom of the muffin tin before pouring in the egg mixture.

PER SERVING (1 MUFFIN): CALORIES: 95; FAT: 6G; SATURATED FAT: 2G; CHOLESTEROL: 190MG; CARBOHYDRATES: 2G; FIBER: <1G; PROTEIN: 8G; SODIUM: 318MG

Everything-Seasoned Avocado Toast with Egg

SERVES 4 • PREP TIME: 5 MINUTES • COOK TIME: 10 MINUTES

Avocado toast is a meal I look forward to eating at least once a week, served alongside a tomato salad. This dish is traditionally made with a fried egg, but I have also used scrambled eggs and poached eggs. I love using everything bagel seasoning on the eggs, but you could substitute red pepper flakes for a little heat.

1 teaspoon extra-virgin olive oil

4 large eggs

1 tablespoon everything bagel seasoning

2 avocados, halved and pitted

½ teaspoon salt

½ teaspoon freshly ground black pepper

4 whole-grain bread slices (I prefer a thick slice), toasted

¼ cup microgreens (optional)

1. In a large nonstick skillet over medium-high, heat the olive oil until hot.

2. One at a time, crack 1 egg into a small bowl. Be sure there is no eggshell in the bowl. Slowly slide the egg from the bowl into the skillet. Sprinkle the eggs with the bagel seasoning and reduce the heat to low. Cook for 5 to 7 minutes, or until the eggs are cooked to your desired doneness.

3. While the eggs cook, scoop the avocado flesh into a small bowl. Add the salt and pepper and mash with a fork until creamy. Spread the toast with the mashed avocado.

4. Place 1 fried egg on each toast and garnish each with 1 tablespoon microgreens (if using).

VARIATION TIP: Create an avocado toast to match your mood. To make it spicy, add some sriracha instead of or with the microgreens. If you want a little cheese, spread some goat cheese on the toast before topping it with the avocado. If you aren't a fan of avocado, mash up leftover sweet potato instead.

PER SERVING: CALORIES: 352; FAT: 22G; SATURATED FAT: 4G; CHOLESTEROL: 186MG; CARBOHYDRATES: 30G; FIBER: 11G; PROTEIN: 14G; SODIUM: 779MG

Tex-Mex Egg White Omelets

SERVES 2 • PREP TIME: 10 MINUTES • COOK TIME: 20 MINUTES

Making omelets with egg whites instead of whole eggs is a great option if you're concerned about cholesterol and calories. Although I enjoy a good egg, I don't feel like I am missing any flavor when I use just the whites.

2¼ teaspoons extra-virgin olive oil, divided

⅓ cup chopped onion

½ red bell pepper, chopped

½ cup sliced mushrooms

¼ cup diced canned green chiles

6 large egg whites, lightly beaten

Salt

Freshly ground black pepper

¼ cup salsa

¼ cup low-fat plain Greek yogurt (optional)

1. In an omelet pan or skillet over medium, heat 1½ teaspoons of olive oil until hot.

2. Add the onion, bell pepper, mushrooms, and green chiles. Sauté for about 5 minutes, or until the vegetables are cooked through. Remove the vegetables from the pan and set aside.

3. Return the pan to the heat and add the remaining ¾ teaspoon of olive oil. Pour in half the egg whites and season with salt and black pepper. Cook for 3 to 4 minutes, or until the whites are set, not runny. Add half the cooked vegetables to one side of the omelet and fold the other side over the filling. Cook for 1 minute more, or until the egg whites are completely cooked through, then transfer to a plate and cover to keep warm. Repeat to make a second omelet.

4. Top the omelets with the salsa and a dollop of yogurt (if using) to serve.

VARIATION TIP: I enjoy this omelet without cheese, but if you are looking for a little more creaminess, a little queso blanco sprinkled in with the vegetables is delicious. If you would like a little extra protein and flavor, add cooked Mexican chorizo and hot sauce.

PER SERVING: CALORIES: 160; FAT: 8G; SATURATED FAT: 1G; CHOLESTEROL: 0MG; CARBOHYDRATES: 11G; FIBER: 3G; PROTEIN: 13G; SODIUM: 383MG

Sun-Dried Tomato & Kale Frittata

SERVES 4 TO 6 • PREP TIME: 10 MINUTES • COOK TIME: 20 MINUTES

Kale—a good source of vitamin C and iron—is one of those dark leafy greens my kids will actually eat. Sun-dried tomatoes are also full of vitamin C and iron, so they make a great match. I love the sweetness and the tart flavor sun-dried tomatoes bring to this dish.

1 tablespoon extra-virgin olive oil

1 cup sliced mushrooms

¼ cup oil-packed sun-dried tomatoes, drained and chopped

¼ cup canned artichoke hearts, drained and chopped

2 cups chopped kale

2 tablespoons chopped fresh parsley

6 large eggs

¼ cup grated Parmesan cheese

½ teaspoon salt

½ teaspoon freshly ground black pepper

1. In a medium, oven-safe nonstick skillet over medium, heat the olive oil until hot.

2. Add the mushrooms, sun-dried tomatoes, and artichoke hearts. Sauté for about 4 minutes, or until the vegetables are softened.

3. Add the kale and parsley. Cook for about 3 minutes more, or until the kale starts to soften.

4. While the vegetables cook, in a large bowl, whisk the eggs, Parmesan cheese, salt, and pepper until combined.

5. Preheat the broiler.

6. Pour the egg mixture into the skillet. Reduce the heat to low, cover the skillet with a lid or aluminum foil, and cook for about 7 minutes, or until the eggs begin to set.

7. Place the skillet under the broiler for about 5 minutes, or until the eggs are cooked and lightly browned.

SERVING TIP: I cut my frittata like a pizza, into 6 wedges, and serve with a salad of microgreens or watercress lightly dressed with oil and vinegar. You can also top the frittata with a dollop of low-fat plain Greek yogurt or goat cheese.

PER SERVING: CALORIES: 215; FAT: 14G; SATURATED FAT: 4G; CHOLESTEROL: 284MG; CARBOHYDRATES: 9G; FIBER: 3G; PROTEIN: 15G; SODIUM: 634MG

Vegetarian Spicy Black Bean Soup

SERVES 4 • PREP TIME: 10 MINUTES • COOK TIME: 15 MINUTES

I love a warm bowl of soup when the weather is chilly. There is something to be said about simmering a stew all day long, but I have made a couple of delicious soups that are ready in much less time. This vegetarian spicy black bean soup is full of flavor. Although great on its own, it's also wonderful as a side dish with a taco dinner.

2 tablespoons extra-virgin olive oil

1 onion, diced

3 garlic cloves, minced

2 (15-ounce) cans low-sodium black beans, rinsed and drained

2 red or yellow bell peppers, chopped

2¼ cups low-sodium vegetable broth

½ cup fresh cilantro or basil, chopped

2 tablespoons balsamic vinegar

1 tablespoon ground cumin

½ teaspoon red pepper flakes

1 avocado, pitted, peeled, and sliced (optional)

1. In a large pot over medium, heat the olive oil until hot. Add the onion and garlic and cook for about 3 minutes, stirring occasionally, or until the onion is translucent.

2. Meanwhile, in a food processor or blender, blend 1 can of black beans until smooth. Pour the puréed beans into the pot, along with the remaining can of whole beans.

3. Stir in the bell peppers, vegetable broth, cilantro, vinegar, cumin, and red pepper flakes. Reduce the heat to medium-low and bring the soup to a simmer. Cook for 10 minutes. Serve the soup topped with the avocado (if using).

VARIATION TIP: Change up the toppings to suit your tastes. Try a dollop of low-fat plain Greek yogurt or a sprinkling of shredded cheese on top. Save your leftovers, as this soup is perfect as a dip for tortilla chips or pita bread as an appetizer.

PER SERVING: CALORIES: 304; FAT: 8G; SATURATED FAT:1G; CHOLESTEROL: 0MG; CARBOHYDRATES: 46G; FIBER: 12G; PROTEIN: 14G; SODIUM: 95MG

Thai Chicken Lettuce Wraps

SERVES 4 • PREP TIME: 10 MINUTES • COOK TIME: 10 MINUTES

I reach for this recipe when I crave takeout. I can make a batch in less time than it takes me to run to the closest Thai restaurant. I use ground chicken, but if you don't have any on hand, cut a chicken breast into small pieces and use that instead.

FOR THE SAUCE

⅓ cup Garlic-Chile Sauce (page 58) or store-bought garlic-chili sauce or sriracha

¼ cup fresh cilantro, chopped

1 tablespoon peanut butter

2 teaspoons low-sodium soy sauce

½ teaspoon grated peeled fresh ginger

FOR THE LETTUCE WRAPS

1 tablespoon sesame oil or extra-virgin olive oil

1 pound ground chicken

4 scallions, white and green parts separated, chopped

3 garlic cloves, minced

1½ cups coleslaw mix

½ teaspoon salt

¼ teaspoon freshly ground black pepper

1 head Bibb lettuce, leaves separated

TO MAKE THE SAUCE

In a small bowl, whisk the garlic-chile sauce, cilantro, peanut butter, soy sauce, and ginger to blend. Set aside.

TO MAKE THE LETTUCE WRAPS

1. In a large skillet over medium, heat the sesame oil. Add the ground chicken, scallion white parts, and garlic. Cook for 5 to 7 minutes, stirring to break up the chicken, or until the chicken is cooked through.

2. Add the coleslaw mix, salt, and pepper. Cook for 2 minutes more.

3. Stir in the sauce. Cook for 1 minute to heat the sauce.

4. Spoon the chicken filling into the lettuce cups and garnish with the scallion green parts.

SUBSTITUTION TIP: Try lean ground beef, ground pork, shrimp, or even tofu in place of the chicken.

PER SERVING: CALORIES: 254; FAT: 15G; SATURATED FAT: 3G; CHOLESTEROL: 105MG; CARBOHYDRATES: 7G; FIBER: 2G; PROTEIN: 25G; SODIUM: 680MG

GETTING SAUCY

Proper seasoning is the key to making healthy eating delicious. To this end, I love to keep my Easy Pesto and Garlic-Chile Sauce in the refrigerator. Neither requires any cooking, and both add a punch of flavor to many of the dishes in this book. Try them on eggs, sandwiches, and grain bowls.

Easy Pesto   MAKES 2 CUPS • PREP TIME: 5 MINUTES

2 cups packed fresh basil leaves

½ cup grated Parmesan cheese

¼ cup pine nuts

1 garlic clove, peeled

Juice of 2 lemons

¼ teaspoon salt

¼ teaspoon freshly ground black pepper

½ cup extra-virgin olive oil

In a food processor, combine the basil, Parmesan cheese, pine nuts, and garlic. Pulse until finely chopped, then add the lemon juice, salt, and pepper. Pulse to combine. With the processor running, slowly add the olive oil and process until a paste-like pesto forms. Keep refrigerated in an airtight container for up to 4 days.

PER ¼-CUP SERVING: CALORIES: 97; FAT: 9G; SATURATED FAT: 2G; CHOLESTEROL: 5MG; CARBOHYDRATES: 2G; FIBER: 1G; PROTEIN: 3G; SODIUM: 190MG

Garlic-Chile Sauce   MAKES 1½ CUPS • PREP TIME: 10 MINUTES

1 cup chopped fresh Thai or serrano chiles

3 garlic cloves, peeled

¼ cup rice vinegar, plus more as needed

1 tablespoon honey or light brown sugar, plus more as needed

1 teaspoon salt

In a food processor, combine the chiles, garlic, vinegar, honey, and salt. Process until smooth. If the sauce seems too thick, add more vinegar a little at a time until you reach your desired consistency. Taste and add more honey, as desired, to tone down the spicy factor. Keep refrigerated in an airtight container for up to 1 month.

PER ¼-CUP SERVING: CALORIES: 17; FAT: <1G; SATURATED FAT: 0G; CHOLESTEROL: 0G; CARBOHYDRATES: 4G; FIBER: 1G; PROTEIN: <1G; SODIUM: 388MG

Grape & Gorgonzola Naan Pizzas

SERVES 4 • PREP TIME: 10 MINUTES • COOK TIME: 10 MINUTES

We frequent a local pizza place that offers a grape pizza. I ordered it one day, and my life hasn't been the same since. If you have never had grapes on a pizza, you need to try it–trust me. This lighter version has a lightly dressed salad on top that rounds it out and makes it a full meal you will love.

1½ cups red seedless grapes, halved lengthwise

6 teaspoons extra-virgin olive oil, divided

4 whole-wheat naan or pita breads

⅔ cup shredded part-skim mozzarella cheese

2 tablespoons (1 ounce) Gorgonzola cheese, crumbled

1 teaspoon chopped fresh rosemary

1 cup baby arugula

1 tablespoon balsamic vinegar

1. Preheat the oven to 425°F.

2. In a small bowl, stir together the grapes and 2 teaspoons of olive oil.

3. Brush the naan with the remaining 4 teaspoons of olive oil. Top the breads with the mozzarella and Gorgonzola cheese.

4. Sprinkle the grapes over the cheese and top with the rosemary. Place the naan pizzas on a baking sheet.

5. Bake for 8 minutes, or until the cheese just starts to brown. Remove from the oven.

6. In a medium bowl, combine the arugula and vinegar. Lightly toss to coat and divide it among the pizzas.

VARIATION TIP: I love stocking up on naan at the grocery store. You can keep them in the freezer and pull them out the morning before making dinner. I use them all the time for different pizza recipes. One of the most fun dinners for my family is when we all make our own pizza and enjoy them with a movie.

PER SERVING: CALORIES: 419; FAT: 19G; SATURATED FAT: 4G; CHOLESTEROL: 15MG; CARBOHYDRATES: 49G; FIBER: 6G; PROTEIN: 14G; SODIUM: 602MG

Quinoa-Zucchini Taco Bowls

SERVES 4 • PREP TIME: 15 MINUTES • COOK TIME: 10 MINUTES

My family regularly enjoys several different versions of tacos, including these quinoa-zucchini taco bowls. Quinoa is gaining popularity, and for good reason. It's an excellent source of magnesium, manganese, and calcium, and it also has twice as much protein as rice, making it a great option for a vegetarian dish. I prep ahead and make a batch on Sunday to use throughout the week, or you can find it already prepared in the grocery store.

1 tablespoon extra-virgin olive oil

2 large zucchini, chopped

1 red bell pepper, chopped

1 yellow bell pepper, chopped

1 onion, chopped

1½ teaspoons chili powder

1½ teaspoons ground cumin

1½ teaspoons sweet or smoked paprika

2 (15-ounce) cans kidney beans or pinto beans

4 cups cooked quinoa, warmed

1 cup salsa

¼ cup low-fat plain Greek yogurt or sour cream (optional)

Chopped fresh cilantro, for garnish (optional)

1 lime, cut into wedges

1. In a large skillet over medium-high, heat the olive oil until hot. Add the zucchini, red bell pepper, yellow bell pepper, and onion. Season with the chili powder, cumin, and paprika. Cook for 3 to 5 minutes, or until the vegetables begin to soften.

2. Stir in the kidney beans and cook for about 5 minutes, or more until the vegetables are tender and the beans are heated through.

3. Divide the quinoa among 4 serving bowls and top with the beans and vegetables.

4. Garnish with the salsa, yogurt (if using), and cilantro (if using). Serve with the lime wedges for squeezing.

VARIATION TIP: To add more vegetarian protein to this dish, include some tofu or tempeh. For a nonvegetarian option, use ground chicken or turkey. This is also a great recipe for leftover turkey.

PER SERVING: CALORIES: 541; FAT: 10G; SATURATED FAT: 1G; CHOLESTEROL: 0MG; CARBOHYDRATES: 89G; FIBER: 22G; PROTEIN: 26G; SODIUM: 1,091MG

Sweet & Spicy Soy-Glazed Tofu

SERVES 4 • PREP TIME: 30 MINUTES • COOK TIME: 15 MINUTES

Don't be intimidated by tofu. It is easy to work with and versatile, and it soaks up the flavors of whatever you cook with it. This recipe is a good tutorial on how to cook it in a skillet. I love some spice in my life, so this dish is on the spicy side, but you can substitute teriyaki sauce or barbecue sauce if you like something with less fire.

½ cup dry sherry

⅓ cup low-sodium soy sauce

2 tablespoons honey

1½ teaspoons red pepper flakes

1 large onion, cut into ¼-inch-thick rounds

1 (12- to 14-ounce) package extra-firm tofu, pressed (see tip) and cut into ½-inch cubes

Cooked rice or noodles

1 tablespoon chopped fresh chives

1. In a small bowl, whisk the sherry, soy sauce, honey, and red pepper flakes to combine.

2. Line a large nonstick skillet with the onion rounds. Place the tofu on top and pour the sauce over everything. Place the skillet over high heat. Cover the skillet and cook for about 5 minutes, or until the mixture begins to boil.

3. Reduce the heat to medium and cook for 5 to 10 minutes more, or until the sauce has thickened and the tofu is heated through. Baste the tofu occasionally with the sauce as it cooks.

4. Serve the tofu over rice, garnished with chives.

INGREDIENT TIP: Extra-firm tofu is great for skillet cooking, deep-frying, or baking. To press tofu, wrap it in paper towels and place something heavy, like a large skillet, on top. Let it sit for 30 minutes. This forces the moisture out of the tofu and helps it absorb flavor better.

PER SERVING: CALORIES: 185; FAT: 4G; SATURATED FAT: 1G; CHOLESTEROL: 0MG; CARBOHYDRATES: 20G; FIBER: 2G; PROTEIN: 11G; SODIUM: 789MG

Use-It-All-Up Leftover Fried Rice

SERVES 4 • PREP TIME: 10 MINUTES • COOK TIME: 15 MINUTES

I've loved fried rice since I learned how to talk. My parents took me to our local Chinese restaurant for special occasions, and I always filled up on rice. After a few days of home-cooked meals, I have a ton of leftovers in the refrigerator. This recipe is perfect for using some of those items–my favorite combination is pancetta with peas.

2 tablespoons canola or vegetable oil, divided

2 cups cooked white rice or brown rice

1 small onion, diced

2 cups frozen diced carrots and peas

3 scallions, thinly sliced on a bias

2 garlic cloves, minced

1 cup diced cooked meat or tofu of choice (see tip)

2 tablespoons low-sodium soy sauce

2 large eggs, lightly beaten

1. In a large nonstick skillet over high, heat 1 tablespoon of canola oil until hot.

2. Add the rice and cook for 3 to 4 minutes, or until the rice starts to brown. Transfer the rice to a bowl and set aside.

3. Reduce the heat to medium-high, return the skillet to the heat, and add the remaining 1 tablespoon of canola oil.

4. Add the onion, carrots and peas, scallions, and garlic. Cook for about 3 minutes, or until the onion is translucent.

5. Stir in the rice to combine.

6. Add the meat and soy sauce. Stir well. Cook for about 2 minutes, or until heated through. Push the rice to side of the skillet and add the eggs. Cook for 2 to 3 minutes, scrambling the eggs. Stir the eggs into the rice mixture.

SUBSTITUTION TIP: This recipe is meant to use up leftovers, so get creative. Try leftover turkey, chicken, pancetta, tofu, or steak. You can change up the vegetables as well. Try frozen broccoli, cooked bell peppers, or leftover cooked sweet potato.

PER SERVING: CALORIES: 331; FAT: 11G; SATURATED FAT: 2G; CHOLESTEROL: 123MG; CARBOHYDRATES: 38G; FIBER: 3G; PROTEIN: 20G; SODIUM: 407MG

Simple Shrimp Scampi with Zucchini

SERVES 4 • PREP TIME: 15 MINUTES • COOK TIME: 15 MINUTES

Shrimp scampi is such a flavorful and easy recipe to make at home, and adding vegetables to pasta dishes is a great way to get more nutrients into your meals.

1 tablespoon salt, plus 1 teaspoon

8 ounces spaghetti

4 tablespoons extra-virgin olive oil, divided

1 large zucchini, quartered and sliced

¼ teaspoon freshly ground black pepper

1 tablespoon butter

4 garlic cloves, minced

1 pound large shrimp, peeled and deveined

1 teaspoon red pepper flakes

¼ cup freshly squeezed lemon juice

¼ cup fresh flat-leaf parsley, chopped

¼ cup grated Romano or Parmesan cheese

1. Bring 4 quarts of water to a boil over high heat. Add 1 tablespoon of salt and the spaghetti. Cook for 8 to 10 minutes, or according to the package directions, until the spaghetti is al dente. Drain. Return the spaghetti to the pot and keep warm.

2. While the spaghetti cooks, in a large skillet over medium-high, heat 2 tablespoons of olive oil until hot.

3. Add the zucchini and season with ½ teaspoon of salt and the black pepper. Cook for about 4 minutes, stirring occasionally, or until tender. Remove the zucchini from the skillet and reserve.

4. Return the skillet to medium-high heat and add the remaining 2 tablespoons of olive oil and the butter to melt. Add the garlic and sauté for 30 seconds. Add the shrimp and season with the remaining ½ teaspoon of salt and the red pepper flakes. Cook for about 2 minutes per side, or until the shrimp are opaque.

5. Stir in the lemon juice and parsley. Add the zucchini and the pasta to the skillet and sprinkle with the Romano cheese. Toss to combine.

PER SERVING: CALORIES: 562; FAT: 26G; SATURATED FAT: 6G; CHOLESTEROL: 239MG; CARBOHYDRATES: 48G; FIBER: 3G; PROTEIN: 39G; SODIUM: 1,343MG

Easy Italian Salmon with Asparagus

SERVES 4 • PREP TIME: 10 MINUTES • COOK TIME: 15 MINUTES

My mom created this recipe using a spice blend she bought from a specialty store. I loved it so much I had to figure out how to make it myself. I think I came close. You can substitute your favorite spices, if you prefer.

Nonstick cooking spray (optional)

1 (1- to 1½-pound) skin-on salmon fillet

1 pound asparagus, woody ends trimmed

3 tablespoons extra-virgin olive oil or melted butter, divided

2 garlic cloves, minced

1 teaspoon grated Romano cheese, plus ¼ cup (¼ cup optional)

1 teaspoon dried basil

1 teaspoon dried parsley

½ teaspoon garlic powder

¼ teaspoon salt

¼ teaspoon freshly ground black pepper

½ lemon

1. Preheat the oven to 400°F. Line a sheet pan with aluminum foil or coat it with cooking spray.

2. Place the salmon on the prepared sheet pan, skin-side down. Arrange the asparagus around the salmon and drizzle the asparagus with 2 tablespoons of olive oil and the garlic.

3. In a small bowl, whisk the remaining 1 tablespoon of olive oil, 1 teaspoon of Romano cheese, the basil, parsley, garlic powder, salt, and pepper to combine. Brush the mixture over the salmon.

4. Depending on the thickness of the salmon, bake for 15 minutes, or until the asparagus is fork-tender and the salmon is cooked through (an internal temperature of 145°F) and flakes easily with a fork. Keep an eye on the salmon to make sure it doesn't burn.

5. Squeeze the lemon over the asparagus, sprinkle with the remaining ¼ cup of Romano cheese (if using), and serve with the salmon.

PER SERVING: CALORIES: 263; FAT: 15G; SATURATED FAT: 3G; CHOLESTEROL: 85MG; CARBOHYDRATES: 8G; FIBER: 3G; PROTEIN: 26G; SODIUM: 204MG

Greek Chicken & Rice Bowl

SERVES 4 • PREP TIME: 15 MINUTES • COOK TIME: 10 MINUTES

Greek flavors snuck up on me: I thought I didn't like them, and then I actually tried them, and I was hooked. I love olives, tomatoes, and feta cheese—and this recipe has them all. This recipe is perfect for lunch or dinner. Serve it with sliced pita bread and hummus if you don't have cooked rice on hand. It is a light meal that fills you up.

1 cup Italian Dressing (page 35), divided

1 pound boneless, skinless chicken breasts, cut into 1-inch pieces

2 cups diced tomato

2 cucumbers, diced

¾ cup pitted Kalamata olives, halved

1 red onion, chopped

1 tablespoon extra-virgin olive oil

½ cup crumbled feta cheese

2 cups cooked brown rice, warmed

1. In a medium bowl, combine ½ cup of Italian dressing and the chicken. Stir to coat and set aside to marinate.

2. In another medium bowl, combine the tomato, cucumbers, olives, and red onion. Set aside.

3. In a large skillet over medium, heat the olive oil until hot. Using a slotted spoon, remove the chicken from the marinade and add it to the skillet. Discard the marinade. Cook the chicken for 5 to 7 minutes, or until cooked through and no longer pink. Set aside.

4. Add the feta cheese to the bowl with the vegetables.

5. Pour the remaining ½ cup of dressing over the vegetables and stir to coat.

6. Place ½ cup brown rice in each of 4 small serving bowls. Top the rice with chicken and evenly divide the vegetable mixture among the bowls.

COOKING TIP: For even more flavor, marinate the chicken overnight in the refrigerator.

PER SERVING: CALORIES: 431; FAT: 20G; SATURATED FAT: 5G; CHOLESTEROL: 82MG; CARBOHYDRATES: 37G; FIBER: 5G; PROTEIN: 30G; SODIUM: 794MG

Easy Chicken Piccata with Cauliflower Rice

SERVES 4 • PREP TIME: 10 MINUTES • COOK TIME: 15 MINUTES

This recipe is the answer to that age-old question, "What can I make with this chicken I have in the refrigerator?" Chicken piccata is a classic dish that is so easy to prepare. Instead of serving it with pasta, I love pairing it with simple cauliflower rice. The extra sauce from the chicken mixes in with the rice and tastes amazing.

⅓ cup whole-wheat flour

1 teaspoon salt

½ teaspoon freshly ground black pepper

2 boneless, skinless chicken breasts, halved lengthwise

2 tablespoons extra-virgin olive oil

1 large lemon, halved, 1 half sliced

2 garlic cloves, minced

1 cup low-sodium chicken broth

1 (10-ounce) package frozen cauliflower rice

2 tablespoons unsalted butter

2 tablespoons capers, drained

Chopped fresh parsley, for garnish (optional)

1. On a plate, stir together the flour, salt, and pepper. Dredge each chicken breast in the seasoned flour and shake off any excess. Discard any leftover flour.

2. In a large cast-iron skillet over medium, heat the olive oil until hot. Add the chicken and panfry for about 3 minutes per side, or until it is browned, cooked through, and no longer pink. Remove the chicken and set aside.

3. Place the lemon slices in the skillet. Cook for about 1 minute. Add the garlic and cook for 30 seconds more. Add the chicken broth and cook for about 3 minutes, or until slightly reduced.

4. While the broth reduces, prepare the cauliflower rice in the microwave according to the package directions.

5. Add the butter, juice from the remaining lemon half, and the capers to the skillet. Stir to combine. Reduce the heat to medium-low.

6. Add the chicken to the skillet and cook for 2 to 3 minutes, or until the chicken is heated through and the sauce is thickened to your liking. Garnish with parsley (if using) and serve with the cauliflower rice.

INGREDIENT TIP: Look for the thin-cut chicken cutlets at the grocery store to save time cutting the chicken.

PER SERVING: CALORIES: 231; FAT: 14G; SATURATED FAT: 5G; CHOLESTEROL: 48MG; CARBOHYDRATES: 14G; FIBER: 4G; PROTEIN: 15G; SODIUM: 1,016MG

Balsamic Chicken & Vegetables with Couscous

I used to make chicken with vegetables and rice so often my kids started complaining, which is when I knew I needed to freshen it up. This variation has a delicious sauce that gives it a lot of flavor. Paired with couscous, it's a nice variation on chicken and rice. Serve this over cauliflower rice to trim the carbs and calories, if you like.

¾ cup Italian Dressing (page 35)

3 tablespoons balsamic vinegar

1 tablespoon honey

¼ teaspoon red pepper flakes

3 tablespoons extra-virgin olive oil, divided

1 pound boneless, skinless chicken breasts, cut into 1-inch pieces

1½ teaspoons salt, divided

½ teaspoon freshly ground black pepper

1¾ cups water

1½ cups couscous

1. In a medium bowl, whisk the Italian dressing, vinegar, honey, and red pepper flakes until well combined. Set aside.

2. In a large skillet over medium-high, heat 2 tablespoons of olive oil until hot. Add the chicken and season it with ½ teaspoon of salt and the black pepper. Cook for about 6 minutes, stirring occasionally, or until the chicken is browned on all sides, cooked through, and no longer pink.

3. While the chicken cooks, bring the water to a boil in a saucepan over medium-high. Add the remaining 1 teaspoon of salt, remaining 1 tablespoon of olive oil, and the couscous. Cover the pan and cook the couscous according to package directions, adjusting the heat as needed. Keep warm.

4. Add half the sauce to the chicken and stir to coat. Using a slotted spoon, transfer the chicken to a bowl, leaving the sauce in the skillet.

1 pound green beans,
  trimmed

1½ cups carrot matchsticks

1 cup grape tomatoes,
  halved, or 1 chopped
  tomato

2 tablespoons fresh basil,
  cut into fine strips
  (optional)

5. Add the green beans, carrots, and tomatoes to the skillet. Cook for about 5 minutes, stirring constantly. I like my vegetables with a little bite, but cook until your desired doneness. Transfer the vegetables to the bowl with the chicken.

6. Add the remaining sauce to the skillet and cook for 1 to 2 minutes, or until it is thickened to your liking. Return the chicken and vegetables to the skillet and toss with the sauce to coat. Serve with the couscous, garnished with the basil (if using).

COOKING TIP: To add more flavor, I use low-sodium chicken broth or vegetable broth instead of the water when I cook couscous in step 3. I often double the couscous needed for a recipe and reserve the leftovers for protein bowls or fried rice later in the week.

PER SERVING: CALORIES: 694; FAT: 35G; SATURATED FAT: 5G; CHOLESTEROL: 65MG; CARBOHYDRATES: 70G; FIBER: 9G; PROTEIN: 34G; SODIUM: 1,539MG

Seared Pork Chops with Mustard Sauce & Steamed Brussels Sprouts

SERVES 4 • PREP TIME: 10 MINUTES • COOK TIME: 20 MINUTES

The star of this dish is the mustard sauce, made after cooking the pork chops. It's slightly sweet from the apple cider and pairs well with the pork. Brussels sprouts are one of my kids' favorite vegetables. I like to capitalize on this liking as much as I can, as they are high in fiber and low in calories.

1 pound Brussels sprouts, trimmed

Salt for seasoning (optional)

1 teaspoon freshly ground black pepper, divided

4 (1-inch-thick) boneless pork chops

1 tablespoon extra-virgin olive oil

2 tablespoons butter, divided

¾ cup low-sodium chicken broth

¼ cup apple cider

2 tablespoons Dijon mustard

1 tablespoon fresh rosemary leaves, chopped

1. Fit a medium saucepan with a steamer. Fill the pan with water up to the bottom of the steamer. Cover the pan and bring the water to a boil. Add the Brussels sprouts. Cover the pan and steam the sprouts for 6 to 8 minutes, or until fork tender. Season with salt, if desired, and ½ teaspoon of pepper.

2. While the Brussels sprouts cook, season the pork chops all over with the remaining ½ teaspoon of pepper and salt, if desired.

3. In a large skillet over medium-high, heat the olive oil and 1 tablespoon of butter. Add the pork chops and cook for 3 to 4 minutes per side, or until the internal temperature reaches 145°F. Remove the chops from the skillet.

4. Return the skillet to the heat and add the chicken broth and apple cider. Bring to a boil. Stir the liquid, scraping up any browned bits from the bottom of the skillet. Reduce the heat to medium-low and simmer the sauce for 5 minutes.

5. Whisk in the mustard, the remaining 1 tablespoon of butter, and the rosemary. Cook for 30 seconds. Return the pork chops to the skillet and cook for 2 to 3 minutes, or until heated through. Place the pork chops on plates, pour the sauce over the meat, and serve with the Brussels sprouts.

SUBSTITUTION TIP: If you don't have apple cider on hand, use white wine or more chicken broth. You can also substitute broccoli or green beans for the Brussels sprouts.

PER SERVING: CALORIES: 290; FAT: 15G; SATURATED FAT: 6G; CHOLESTEROL: 71MG; CARBOHYDRATES: 13G; FIBER: 5G; PROTEIN: 25G; SODIUM: 866MG

Chicken Sausage & Vegetable Skillet Meal

SERVES 4 • PREP TIME: 15 MINUTES • COOK TIME: 15 MINUTES

This is one of the most popular recipes in our household, not only because it is so easy to make, but also because it is so good. This is a great recipe for using up any vegetables you have in the refrigerator. I have made it with zucchini, corn, and broccoli. When we are on a tight schedule, I use a bag of frozen stir-fry vegetables; this little trick turns it into a 20-minute meal.

1 tablespoon extra-virgin olive oil

½ onion, diced

½ red bell pepper, sliced

½ green bell pepper, sliced

½ cup sliced mushrooms

½ cup sliced water chestnuts

1 teaspoon garlic powder

½ teaspoon salt

½ teaspoon freshly ground black pepper

1 (12-ounce) package smoked chicken sausage (I love the apple flavor), cut into ½-inch-thick pieces

1. In a large skillet over medium heat, warm the olive oil. Add the onion, red bell pepper, green bell pepper, mushrooms, and water chestnuts. Season with garlic powder, salt, and black pepper. Cook for about 7 minutes, stirring occasionally, or until the vegetables are tender. Transfer the vegetables to a bowl.

2. Return the skillet to the heat and arrange the sausage pieces in the skillet. Cook for about 4 minutes per side to brown and cook through. Stir the vegetables into the skillet. Cook for 1 to 2 minutes, or until the vegetables are hot.

LOVE YOUR LEFTOVERS: I highly suggest making a double batch, because the leftovers taste amazing. I also love to cut the sausage and vegetables into smaller pieces and make an omelet with them in the morning.

PER SERVING: CALORIES: 348; FAT: 22G; SATURATED FAT: 7G; CHOLESTEROL: 105MG; CARBOHYDRATES: 18G; FIBER: 2G; PROTEIN: 22G; SODIUM: 1719MG

Seared Steak with Garlic Mushrooms & Sautéed Spinach

SERVES 4 • PREP TIME: 10 MINUTES • COOK TIME: 15 MINUTES

I hope the last meal I ever eat is steak and potatoes. This dinner is the one I choose every birthday and special occasion. The earthy mushrooms pair nicely with the steak, and a side of greens rounds out the meal, fit for any special night in.

4 (1-inch-thick) sirloin steaks (1 to 1½ pounds)

1 teaspoon salt, divided

½ teaspoon freshly ground black pepper, divided

2 tablespoons extra-virgin olive oil, divided

1 tablespoon butter

4 garlic cloves, minced

8 ounces mushrooms, sliced

6 cups fresh baby spinach

Chopped fresh parsley, for garnish

1. Pat the steaks dry with a paper towel and season both sides with ½ teaspoon of salt and ¼ teaspoon of pepper.

2. In a large skillet over medium-high, heat 1 tablespoon of olive oil and the butter to melt. Add the steaks and cook for 4 minutes per side for medium, or until they reach your desired doneness. Remove from the skillet and let rest.

3. Return the skillet to the stovetop and reduce the heat to medium. Heat the remaining 1 tablespoon of olive oil.

4. Add the garlic and cook for 20 seconds. Add the mushrooms and cook for about 2 minutes, stirring occasionally, or until the mushrooms begin to soften.

5. Stir in the spinach and cook for about 4 minutes, or until it wilts. Serve the vegetables with the steaks. Garnish with parsley.

INGREDIENT TIP: Look for steamable red potatoes you can make in the microwave. These are great with steak and can be ready in about 10 minutes.

PER SERVING: CALORIES: 358; FAT: 26G; SATURATED FAT: 9G; CHOLESTEROL: 83MG; CARBOHYDRATES: 5G; FIBER: 2G; PROTEIN: 26G; SODIUM: 717MG

Flank Steak with Chimichurri

SERVES 4 TO 6 • PREP TIME: 15 MINUTES • COOK TIME: 15 MINUTES

I was looking for a new steak recipe when I learned about chimichurri, a full-flavored herb pesto that originated in Argentina. This chimichurri gives the steak the extra flavor punch a lean meat needs. If you are looking to change up an old favorite, this recipe is for you.

FOR THE CHIMICHURRI

½ cup fresh cilantro leaves

½ cup fresh parsley leaves

½ onion, diced

⅓ cup extra-virgin olive oil

Juice of 3 limes

1 tablespoon minced garlic

1 teaspoon salt

½ teaspoon dried oregano

½ teaspoon red pepper flakes

¼ teaspoon freshly ground black pepper

FOR THE FLANK STEAK

1 to 1½ pounds flank steak, trimmed

¼ cup Montreal steak seasoning

1 tablespoon extra-virgin olive oil

TO MAKE THE CHIMICHURRI

In a food processor, combine the cilantro, parsley, onion, olive oil, lime juice, garlic, salt, oregano, red pepper flakes, and black pepper. Pulse until smooth, stopping to scrape down the sides as needed. Set aside.

TO MAKE THE FLANK STEAK

1. Preheat a grill to medium-high heat or a grill pan over medium-high heat.

2. Pat dry the flank steak with a paper towel and rub it all over with the seasoning.

3. Rub the grill with the olive oil and place the steak on the grill. Cook to your desired level of doneness, which for medium is about 4 to 6 minutes per side, or until the center is light pink in color or reaches a minimum internal temperature of 145°F. Transfer the steak to a cutting board and let rest for 5 minutes.

4. Thinly slice the steak against the grain and serve with the chimichurri.

PER SERVING: CALORIES: 401; FAT: 29G; SATURATED FAT: 3G; CHOLESTEROL: 45MG; CARBOHYDRATES: 7G; FIBER: 1G; PROTEIN: 25G; SODIUM: 996MG

Simple Beef Stir-Fry

SERVES 4 • PREP TIME: 15 MINUTES • COOK TIME: 15 MINUTES

 This stir-fry is a great recipe if you have picky eaters, like I do. I use beef here, but you can easily substitute chicken, pork, or even tofu.

¼ cup low-sodium soy sauce

2 tablespoons rice vinegar

2 tablespoons freshly squeezed orange juice

2 tablespoons honey

2 teaspoons sesame oil

1 pound flank steak, sirloin, or skirt steak, thinly sliced against the grain into ½-inch strips

½ teaspoon salt

½ teaspoon freshly ground black pepper

2 tablespoons extra-virgin olive oil, divided

2 garlic cloves, minced

1 red bell pepper, cut into thin strips

1 yellow bell pepper, cut into thin strips

3 cups sugar snap peas, trimmed

2 tablespoons sesame seeds

1. In a small bowl, whisk the soy sauce, vinegar, orange juice, honey, and sesame oil until combined. Set aside.

2. Season the steak on both sides with the salt and black pepper.

3. In a large skillet over medium-high, heat 1 tablespoon of olive oil until hot.

4. Working in batches as needed, add the steak to the skillet in a single layer. Sauté for about 3 minutes per side, or until cooked through. Remove the steak, cover to keep warm, and set aside.

5. Return the skillet to the stovetop and reduce the heat to medium. Add the remaining 1 tablespoon of olive oil to the skillet. When the oil is hot, add the garlic and cook for 30 seconds. Add the red bell pepper, yellow bell pepper, and snap peas to the skillet. Cook for about 4 minutes, or until the vegetables are just softened.

6. Return the steak to the skillet and pour in the sauce. Toss the vegetables and meat with the sauce until coated. Cook for 2 to 3 minutes more, or until the steak is heated through.

7. Sprinkle with the sesame seeds and serve.

PER SERVING: CALORIES: 385; FAT: 19G; SATURATED FAT: 2G; CHOLESTEROL: 45MG; CARBOHYDRATES: 24G; FIBER: 4G; PROTEIN: 29G; SODIUM: 933MG

PORK CHOPS WITH COLLARD GREENS, PAGE 96

CHAPTER FIVE

One-Pot and Skillet Meals

Easy Potato Breakfast Hash

SERVES 4 • PREP TIME: 15 MINUTES • COOK TIME: 20 MINUTES

Potatoes—I can't live without them. They get a bad rap these days, but they are full of heart-healthy ingredients, including fiber, so don't discount them. My favorite pairing is potatoes with eggs. This breakfast hash combines some of my beloved breakfast foods in one skillet.

2 tablespoons extra-virgin olive oil

1 pound potatoes, butternut squash, or sweet potatoes, diced

8 ounces baby bella mushrooms, sliced

1 cup Brussels sprouts, halved

1 red bell pepper, diced

3 cups fresh baby spinach

Salt

Freshly ground black pepper

4 large eggs

Fresh thyme leaves, for garnish (optional)

1. In a large skillet over medium-high, heat the olive oil until hot.

2. Add the potatoes and cook for about 4 minutes.

3. Add the mushrooms, Brussels sprouts, and bell pepper. Cook for 6 to 8 minutes, or until the potatoes are tender.

4. Add the spinach and season with salt and black pepper. Cook for about 2 minutes, or until the spinach wilts.

5. Move the mixture around in the skillet and make 4 wells in it. Crack 1 egg into each well. Cover the skillet and cook for about 5 minutes for medium eggs, or until the eggs are cooked to your desired doneness. Serve garnished with fresh thyme (if using).

VARIATION TIP: This recipe is perfect for using up leftovers in your refrigerator. Add a handful of diced cooked ham or shredded cooked turkey. I have even thrown in leftover taco meat. It was delicious.

PER SERVING: CALORIES: 250; FAT: 12G; SATURATED FAT: 3G; CHOLESTEROL: 186MG; CARBOHYDRATES: 26G; FIBER: 6G; PROTEIN: 12G; SODIUM: 133MG

Sausage, Kale & Quinoa Breakfast Skillet

SERVES 4 TO 6 • PREP TIME: 10 MINUTES • COOK TIME: 35 MINUTES

I call this a breakfast skillet because I enjoy making it the night before and eating it first thing the next morning. It is filled with protein and vegetables to give you energy throughout the day. It also makes a lovely option for lunch or dinner.

1 tablespoon extra-virgin olive oil

3 garlic cloves, minced

1 zucchini, chopped

1 pound fully cooked chicken sausage (I love andouille), cut into rounds

4 cups chopped kale

1 cup frozen corn

1 cup quinoa, rinsed well

1 cup apple cider

1 cup low-sodium chicken broth

¼ cup grated Parmesan cheese

1. In a large, deep skillet over medium-high, heat the olive oil until hot.

2. Add the garlic and sauté for 30 seconds. Add the zucchini and sausage and cook for about 6 minutes, stirring occasionally, or until the sausage is browned on both sides. Add the kale and sauté for 1 minute, or until the kale begins to wilt.

3. Stir in the corn, quinoa, apple cider, and chicken broth. Bring to a boil. Reduce the heat to low and cover the skillet. Simmer the mixture for 20 to 25 minutes, or until the quinoa has absorbed all the liquid.

4. Sprinkle with Parmesan cheese and serve. Refrigerate leftovers in an airtight container for up to 4 days.

VARIATION TIP: Other meats would also make a tasty meal. Try slices of beef left over from a steak dinner with some mushrooms instead of zucchini.

PER SERVING: CALORIES: 579; FAT: 25G; SATURATED FAT: 7G; CHOLESTEROL: 118MG; CARBOHYDRATES: 62G; FIBER: 9G; PROTEIN: 30G; SODIUM: 1,028MG

Carrot Ginger Soup

SERVES 4 TO 6 • PREP TIME: 20 MINUTES • COOK TIME: 35 MINUTES

Ginger is a multitalented ingredient: In addition to tasting great, it can soothe sore muscles and help reduce inflammation, so this recipe is especially good for a post-workout lunch. This is a good dish to make ahead and freeze for later meals.

1 tablespoon unsalted butter

2 pounds carrots, diced (5 cups)

1 onion, chopped

3 garlic cloves, minced

2 tablespoons chopped peeled fresh ginger

1 teaspoon salt

½ teaspoon freshly ground black pepper

½ teaspoon ground turmeric

4 cups low-sodium vegetable broth or low-sodium chicken broth

1 cup coconut milk

Low-fat plain Greek yogurt, for garnish (optional)

1. In a large Dutch oven or stockpot over medium, melt the butter.

2. Add the carrots, onion, and garlic. Cook for about 8 minutes, stirring occasionally, until the onion is translucent.

3. Stir in the ginger, salt, pepper, and turmeric. Cook for about 2 minutes.

4. Stir in the vegetable broth and bring the soup to a simmer. Cook for 20 to 25 minutes, until the carrots are soft.

5. Using an immersion blender, blend the soup to your desired consistency.

6. Stir in the coconut milk. Serve garnished with a dollop of yogurt (if using). Refrigerate leftovers in an airtight container for up to 4 days.

COOKING TIP: If you don't have an immersion blender, use a regular blender, working in batches as needed.

PER SERVING: CALORIES: 230; FAT: 14G; SATURATED FAT: 11G; CHOLESTEROL: 8MG; CARBOHYDRATES: 24G; FIBER: 6G; PROTEIN: 3G; SODIUM: 849MG

Quinoa Vegetable Soup

SERVES 4 TO 6 • PREP TIME: 15 MINUTES • COOK TIME: 40 MINUTES

My favorite soups usually contain a ton of vegetables, because I love the flavor. The quinoa adds plenty of protein and fiber to keep you feeling full and satisfied throughout the day. I love the texture it brings to this otherwise traditional vegetable soup.

2 tablespoons extra-virgin olive oil

1 onion, chopped

4 garlic cloves, minced

3 carrots, sliced

2 celery stalks, diced

1 zucchini, diced

1 (14.5-ounce) can diced tomatoes

¾ cup quinoa, rinsed well

2 teaspoons Italian seasoning

6 cups low-sodium vegetable broth

1 cup chopped kale or fresh spinach

Salt

Freshly ground black pepper

1. In a large Dutch oven or stockpot over medium-high, heat the olive oil until hot.

2. Add the onion, garlic, carrots, celery, and zucchini. Cook for 8 to 9 minutes, until the vegetables are tender.

3. Stir in the tomatoes, quinoa, Italian seasoning, and vegetable broth. Bring the soup to a boil. Reduce the heat, cover the pot, and simmer for 20 to 25 minutes, until the quinoa is cooked.

4. Stir in the kale and cook for 5 minutes more. Taste and season with salt and pepper. Refrigerate leftovers in an airtight container for up to 4 days.

VARIATION TIP: Add 1 can of beans (any type you like) with the tomatoes for a heartier, stew-like soup.

PER SERVING: CALORIES: 289; FAT: 10G; SATURATED FAT: 1G; CHOLESTEROL: 0MG; CARBOHYDRATES: 44G; FIBER: 8G; PROTEIN: 8G; SODIUM: 466MG

Tomato Soup with Basil Oil

SERVES 4 TO 6 • PREP TIME: 10 MINUTES • COOK TIME: 30 MINUTES

When it is rainy or cloudy outside, you will often find my family indoors enjoying tomato soup. This one is garnished with basil oil, which gives it a beautiful, fragrant, tasty finish. You can skip the basil oil, of course, but do throw in a couple basil leaves before blending.

7 tablespoons extra-virgin olive oil, divided

1 onion, diced

3 garlic cloves, minced

5 (14.5-ounce) cans diced tomatoes

Salt

1 cup fresh basil leaves

Juice of ½ lemon

Freshly ground black pepper

1. In a large Dutch oven or stockpot over medium-high, heat 1 tablespoon of olive oil until hot.

2. Add the onion and garlic. Cook for about 5 minutes, stirring occasionally, or until the onion is translucent.

3. Add the tomatoes to the pot and bring the soup to a boil. Reduce the heat and simmer for about 20 minutes.

4. While the soup simmers, in a blender, combine the remaining 6 tablespoons of olive oil, the basil leaves, and lemon juice. Blend until puréed. Set aside.

5. Using an immersion blender, blend the soup in the pot to your desired consistency. Taste and season with salt and pepper. Serve the soup with a drizzle of basil oil on top.

6. Refrigerate leftovers in an airtight container for up to 4 days.

INGREDIENT TIP: I use canned tomatoes here because I keep them stocked in my pantry at all times, but you can absolutely make this soup with fresh tomatoes. You will need about 8 cups halved, cored, and seeded tomatoes. You may have to cook the soup a little longer to break down the tomatoes.

PER SERVING: CALORIES: 338; FAT: 25G; SATURATED FAT: 4G; CHOLESTEROL: 0MG; CARBOHYDRATES: 22G; FIBER: 5G; PROTEIN: 5G; SODIUM: 964MG

Wild Rice Soup

SERVES 6 • PREP TIME: 15 MINUTES • COOK TIME: 1 HOUR

Wild rice is high in fiber and protein, making it an excellent vegetarian choice. I am a huge fan of mushrooms, which are delicious and full of anti-oxidants. In other words, this soup not only tastes fantastic and fills you up, but it is also great for your overall health. I enjoy this soup with whole milk, but use half-and-half if you want to make it a little richer.

2 tablespoons extra-virgin olive oil

8 ounces baby bella mushrooms, sliced

1 onion, diced

1 cup diced carrots (about 2 carrots)

½ cup diced celery (about 2 stalks)

4 garlic cloves, minced

6 cups low-sodium vegetable broth or low-sodium chicken broth

1½ cups wild rice

1 bay leaf

1 cup whole milk or half-and-half

Salt

Freshly ground black pepper

Fresh thyme leaves, for garnish (optional)

1. In a large Dutch oven or stockpot over medium-high, heat the olive oil until hot.

2. Add the mushrooms, onion, carrots, and celery. Cook for about 5 minutes, stirring occasionally, or until the vegetables have softened. Add the garlic and cook for 1 minute more.

3. Stir in the vegetable broth, wild rice, and bay leaf. Bring the soup to a boil. Reduce the heat to a simmer and cook, uncovered, for 45 minutes to 1 hour, or until the rice is tender.

4. Remove the pot from the heat and stir in the milk. Taste and season with salt and pepper. Serve garnished with thyme (if using). Refrigerate leftovers in an airtight container for up to 4 days.

INGREDIENT TIP: I use baby bella mushrooms in this recipe because they are widely available in most grocery stores, but you can use any type of mushroom you like. Each type of mushroom will give the soup a slightly different flavor.

PER SERVING: CALORIES: 280; FAT: 6G; SATURATED FAT: 2G; CHOLESTEROL: 5MG; CARBOHYDRATES: 46G; FIBER: 5G; PROTEIN: 9G; SODIUM: 192MG

Chicken Tortilla Soup

SERVES 4 TO 6 • PREP TIME: 15 MINUTES • COOK TIME: 35 MINUTES

This is my favorite recipe to make when I have leftover rotisserie chicken in the refrigerator. You get the same flavors as in a taco, but in a warm, hearty soup that's perfect any day of the week. My kids don't appreciate spicy foods like my husband and I do, so when we make this for just us, we add some hot sauce or red pepper flakes.

2 tablespoons extra-virgin olive oil

1 large onion, chopped

3 garlic cloves, minced

4 cups low-sodium chicken broth

1 (14.5-ounce) can diced tomatoes

1 (15-ounce) can low-sodium black beans, rinsed and drained

1 (1-ounce) packet taco seasoning

1½ cups shredded cooked chicken

1 cup frozen corn

Salt

Freshly ground black pepper

Shredded cheese of choice, for garnish (optional)

1 cup crushed tortilla chips

Fresh cilantro, for garnish (optional)

1. In a large Dutch oven or stockpot over medium, heat the olive oil until hot.

2. Add the onion and cook for 5 minutes. Add the garlic and cook for 2 minutes more, or until the onion is translucent.

3. Stir in the chicken broth, tomatoes, black beans, and taco seasoning. Bring the soup to a boil, then stir in the chicken. Reduce the heat to low and simmer the soup for 15 minutes.

4. Stir in the corn. Taste and season with salt and pepper. Cook the soup for about 6 minutes more, or until the corn is heated through.

5. Garnish each serving with cheese (if using), the tortilla chips, and cilantro (if using). Refrigerate leftovers in an airtight container for up to 4 days.

SUBSTITUTION TIP: You can make your own taco seasoning. In a small bowl, whisk 2 tablespoons chili powder, 2 teaspoons ground cumin, ½ teaspoon ground coriander, and ½ teaspoon garlic powder. Store leftovers in an airtight container.

PER SERVING: CALORIES: 431; FAT: 13G; SATURATED FAT: 2G; CHOLESTEROL: 45MG; CARBOHYDRATES: 49G; FIBER: 8G; PROTEIN: 28G; SODIUM: 830MG

Sweet Potato & Black Bean Chili

SERVES 6 • PREP TIME: 10 MINUTES • COOK TIME: 40 MINUTES

This chili is tasty, nutritious, and perfect for a crisp fall day. Filled with black beans, sweet potatoes, and corn, this is my go-to chili recipe. This recipe is vegetarian, but you could easily add ground beef, chicken, or turkey if you want meat protein. Serve with your favorite toppings—I suggest shredded cheese and plain Greek yogurt.

1 tablespoon extra-virgin olive oil

2 sweet potatoes, peeled and diced

1 large onion, diced

3 garlic cloves, minced

2 tablespoons chili powder

1 tablespoon ground cumin

2 cups water

1 (8-ounce) can tomato sauce

1 cup frozen corn

1 (15-ounce) can low-sodium black beans, rinsed and drained

1 tablespoon freshly squeezed lime juice

1. In a large Dutch oven or stockpot over medium-high, heat the olive oil until hot. Add the sweet potatoes and onion. Cook for about 8 minutes, stirring occasionally, or until the sweet potatoes start to soften and the onion turns translucent.

2. Stir in the garlic, chili powder, and cumin.

3. Add the water, tomato sauce, and corn. Bring the soup to a simmer and adjust the heat as needed. Cook for about 15 minutes, or until the sweet potatoes are tender.

4. Stir in the black beans and lime juice. Return the soup to a simmer and cook for about 10 minutes more, or until the flavors meld.

LOVE YOUR LEFTOVERS: Refrigerate leftovers in an airtight container for up to 4 days. Better yet, make a double batch and freeze for meals in a snap—the chili reheats beautifully.

PER SERVING: CALORIES: 194; FAT: 4G; SATURATED FAT: 1G; CHOLESTEROL: 0MG; CARBOHYDRATES: 36G; FIBER: 8G; PROTEIN: 7G; SODIUM: 260MG

Rigatoni with Tomatoes & Spinach

SERVES 6 • PREP TIME: 10 MINUTES • COOK TIME: 30 MINUTES

This simple pasta is easy to make and has very little cleanup, thanks to the one-pot method. I sometimes add some red pepper flakes while the garlic cooks. You can also add meat—it is great with either chicken or salmon.

1 tablespoon extra-virgin olive oil

1 onion, chopped

5 garlic cloves, minced

3 cups rigatoni

1 (14.5-ounce) can diced tomatoes

1½ cups low-sodium chicken broth

½ teaspoon dried basil

1 cup halved cherry tomatoes

1 (10-ounce) bag fresh spinach

¼ cup grated Parmesan cheese

1. In a large saucepan over medium-high, heat the olive oil until hot.

2. Add the onion and garlic. Cook for about 4 minutes, stirring occasionally, or until the onion is translucent.

3. Add the rigatoni, diced tomatoes, chicken broth, and basil to the pan and stir to combine. Bring to a boil, then reduce the heat to a simmer and cook for about 15 minutes, or until the rigatoni is almost al dente.

4. Stir in the cherry tomatoes and spinach. Reduce the heat to low. Cook for 3 to 4 minutes, or until the spinach is wilted. Serve sprinkled with the Parmesan cheese. Refrigerate leftovers in an airtight container for up to 3 days.

SUBSTITUTION TIP: Use any type of pasta you have on hand. Consult the package and adjust your cooking time as needed.

PER SERVING: CALORIES: 285; FAT: 5G; SATURATED FAT: 1G; CHOLESTEROL: 3MG; CARBOHYDRATES: 50G; FIBER: 4G; PROTEIN: 12G; SODIUM: 263MG

Smoked Salmon & Asparagus Fettuccine

SERVES 4 TO 6 • PREP TIME: 15 MINUTES • COOK TIME: 40 MINUTES

My husband used to serve homemade smoked salmon every Thanksgiving. It was so delicious, but nowadays we enjoy store-bought smoked salmon. It's great with pasta: The smoky flavor of the fish pairs really well with a creamy yogurt sauce.

2 tablespoons extra-virgin olive oil, divided

2 garlic cloves, minced

1 onion, diced

1 cup chopped asparagus

4 cups low-sodium vegetable broth, divided

8 ounces dried fettuccine

1 cup chopped kale

1 cup low-fat plain Greek yogurt

1 tablespoon capers, drained

8 ounces smoked salmon, chopped

Salt

Freshly ground black pepper

1 tablespoon chopped fresh chives (optional)

1. In a large skillet over medium, heat 1 tablespoon of olive oil until hot.

2. Add the garlic, onion, and asparagus. Sauté for about 7 minutes, or until the asparagus is tender. Remove the vegetables from the skillet, cover, and set aside.

3. Add 3 cups of vegetable broth to the skillet and bring it to a simmer over high heat.

4. Stir in the fettuccine. Reduce the heat to a simmer and cook for 15 minutes.

5. Add the kale and cook for about 10 minutes more, or until the fettuccine is al dente.

6. Reduce the heat to low and stir in the yogurt and capers until the fettuccine is coated with the sauce. If you need to thin the sauce, pour in the remaining 1 cup of vegetable broth, a tablespoon or two at a time, until the sauce reaches the desired consistency.

7. Return the vegetables to the skillet, add the salmon, and stir to combine. Cook for 3 to 4 minutes, or until heated. Taste and season with salt and pepper. Serve garnished with the chives (if using).

PER SERVING: CALORIES: 404; FAT: 12G; SATURATED FAT: 2G; CHOLESTEROL: 22MG; CARBOHYDRATES: 52G; FIBER: 4G; PROTEIN: 24G; SODIUM: 1,340MG

Easy Coconut Curry Shrimp

SERVES 4 TO 6 • PREP TIME: 20 MINUTES • COOK TIME: 15 MINUTES

Fish sauce is a flavorful, pungent sauce common in Southeast Asian cuisine. It adds a nice salty flavor to this curry. Fish sauce also contains all the good nutrients and minerals you find in fish, like iodine and vitamins A and D.

2 tablespoons extra-virgin olive oil

1 onion, minced

4 garlic cloves, minced

2 teaspoons minced fresh ginger

½ teaspoon red pepper flakes, more or less as desired

1 tablespoon curry powder

1 cup coconut milk

1 tablespoon fish sauce or low-sodium soy sauce

1½ pounds large shrimp, peeled and deveined

Salt

Freshly ground black pepper

½ cup fresh cilantro leaves (optional)

2 cups cooked white or brown rice, warmed

1. In a large skillet over medium, heat the olive oil until hot.

2. Add the onion, garlic, ginger, and red pepper flakes. Cook for about 4 minutes, stirring frequently, or until the onion is translucent. Stir in the curry powder until combined.

3. Add the coconut milk and fish sauce. Cook for about 5 minutes, or until the sauce starts to reduce.

4. Add the shrimp and cook for about 5 minutes, stirring frequently, or until the shrimp turn pink. Taste and season with salt and pepper.

5. Turn off the heat, stir in the cilantro (if using), and serve the shrimp and sauce over the rice. Refrigerate leftovers in an airtight container for up to 3 days.

SUBSTITUTION TIP: You can substitute 2 tablespoons red or green curry paste for the curry powder, which might add a bit more spice.

PER SERVING: CALORIES: 510; FAT: 21G; SATURATED FAT: 10G; CHOLESTEROL: 340MG; CARBOHYDRATES: 33G; FIBER: 1G; PROTEIN: 46G; SODIUM: 1,285MG

Pan-Seared Tilapia with Pesto & Tomatoes

SERVES 4 TO 6 • PREP TIME: 10 MINUTES • COOK TIME: 10 MINUTES

Attention, hesitant fish eaters: This recipe is so tasty you'll want to make it all the time. I use homemade pesto, but you could easily cut out that step and substitute your favorite store-bought brand. I enjoy serving this recipe with a side of brown rice or couscous.

4 to 6 tilapia fillets (about 1½ pounds)

½ teaspoon paprika

½ teaspoon salt

¼ teaspoon freshly ground black pepper

2 cups arugula

2 tablespoons extra-virgin olive oil

1 tablespoon butter

4 to 6 tablespoons Easy Pesto (page 58)

1 cup halved grape tomatoes

1 lemon

1. Season each fillet with the paprika, salt, and pepper. Set aside.

2. Divide the arugula among serving plates, and set aside.

3. In a large skillet over medium, heat the olive oil until hot. Add the butter to melt.

4. Add the seasoned fillets to the skillet and sear each side for 3 to 4 minutes, or until done. Transfer the fillets to the bed of arugula.

5. Top each fillet with 1 tablespoon of pesto. Place the halved tomatoes on top of the pesto and squeeze the lemon on top. Refrigerate leftovers in an airtight container for up to 2 days.

SUBSTITUTION TIP: This recipe can be made with a variety of fish. Try trout, cod, red snapper, or salmon.

PER SERVING: CALORIES: 289; FAT: 15G; SATURATED FAT: 4G; CHOLESTEROL: 96MG; CARBOHYDRATES: 4G; FIBER: 1G; PROTEIN: 36G; SODIUM: 455MG

Easy Jambalaya with Sausage & Shrimp

SERVES 4 TO 6 • PREP TIME: 15 MINUTES • COOK TIME: 45 MINUTES

Jambalaya can be made several ways. This Creole version is simple yet packs a lot of flavor. Adjust the seasonings and the type of sausage to make it as spicy as you like. I use chicken sausage because my kids like it, but try andouille for a little kick.

2 tablespoons extra-virgin olive oil, divided

1 (13-ounce) package smoked chicken or turkey sausage, cut into rounds

1 onion, chopped

1 bell pepper, any color, chopped

2 garlic cloves, minced

2 teaspoons Creole seasoning

1 cup brown rice

1 (15-ounce) can tomato sauce

2 cups low-sodium chicken broth

8 ounces shrimp, peeled and deveined

Salt

Freshly ground black pepper

1. In a large Dutch oven, deep sauté pan, or skillet over medium-high, heat 1 tablespoon of olive oil until hot. Add the sausage and cook for about 4 minutes per side, or until browned. Remove the sausage from the pan and set aside.

2. Add the remaining 1 tablespoon of olive oil to the pan along with the onion, bell pepper, and garlic. Cook for 4 to 5 minutes, or until softened, stirring to scrape up all the browned bits from the bottom of the pan.

3. Stir in the Creole seasoning and brown rice. Add the tomato sauce and chicken broth and bring the mixture to a boil. Reduce the heat to a simmer and cook, covered, for 40 to 50 minutes, stirring occasionally, or until the rice is tender.

4. Add the shrimp and cook for 5 to 6 minutes, or until opaque and pink. Taste and season with salt and black pepper. Refrigerate leftovers in an air-tight container for up to 3 days.

PER SERVING: CALORIES: 529; FAT: 22G; SATURATED FAT: 5G; CHOLESTEROL: 149MG; CARBOHYDRATES: 56G; FIBER: 5G; PROTEIN: 31G; SODIUM: 2,307MG

Chicken Pad Thai with Zoodles

SERVES 4 TO 6 • PREP TIME: 20 MINUTES • COOK TIME: 25 MINUTES

Whenever we go to a Thai restaurant, my husband always orders the pad Thai. My version, made with zoodles, is healthier and easy to make at home. We use our favorite store-bought pad Thai sauce.

2 tablespoons extra-virgin olive oil, divided

1 pound boneless, skinless chicken breasts, cut into 1-inch pieces

Salt

Freshly ground black pepper

2 red bell peppers, thinly sliced

2 carrots, shredded

2 large eggs, beaten

6 large zucchini, spiralized

1 cup bean sprouts

1 cup store-bought pad Thai sauce

¼ cup sliced scallions

¼ cup crushed peanuts (optional)

1. In a large saucepan over medium, heat 1 tablespoon of olive oil until hot.

2. Season the chicken all over with salt and black pepper and add it to the pan. Cook for 4 to 8 minutes, stirring occasionally, or until browned and cooked through. Remove the chicken from the pan and set aside.

3. Return the pan to the heat and add the remaining 1 tablespoon of olive oil, the bell peppers, and carrots. Cook for 4 to 5 minutes, or until softened. Push the vegetables to one side of the pan and pour the eggs into the other side. Scramble the eggs until they're cooked to your desired doneness, then stir them into the vegetables.

4. Add the zucchini, bean sprouts, and pad Thai sauce. Stir to combine.

5. Add the chicken and scallions. Cook for about 5 minutes, or until heated through and the zoodles are cooked but not mushy. Top with the crushed peanuts (if using) and serve.

6. Refrigerate leftovers in an airtight container for 2 to 3 days.

PER SERVING: CALORIES: 443; FAT: 15G; SATURATED FAT: 3G; CHOLESTEROL: 158MG; CARBOHYDRATES: 53G; FIBER: 8G; PROTEIN: 34G; SODIUM: 1,888MG

Lemon Pepper Chicken with Broccoli

SERVES 4 • PREP TIME: 15 MINUTES • COOK TIME: 15 MINUTES

This light meal has tons of bright flavor thanks to the lemon zest–and all members of the family will enjoy it. Serve over your favorite cooked pasta for a heartier dinner, if you like.

1 tablespoon extra-virgin olive oil

1½ pounds boneless, skinless chicken breast cutlets

2 teaspoons lemon pepper

1 teaspoon salt

⅓ cup low-sodium chicken broth

Zest of 1 lemon

3 tablespoons freshly squeezed lemon juice

3 cups broccoli florets

1. Preheat the oven to 400°F.

2. In a large, oven-safe skillet over medium, heat the olive oil until hot.

3. Season the chicken on both sides with the lemon pepper and salt. Place the chicken in the skillet and cook for about 2 minutes per side, or until browned.

4. In a small bowl, whisk the chicken broth with the lemon zest and juice to combine. Pour the mixture over the chicken.

5. Arrange the broccoli around the chicken and place the skillet in the oven.

6. Roast for about 10 minutes, or until the chicken reaches an internal temperature of 165°F.

COOKING TIP: I love buying thinly sliced chicken breasts at the grocery store, but if you can't find them or you already have regular chicken breasts in the refrigerator, halve them lengthwise and pound them until about ½ inch thick.

PER SERVING: CALORIES: 225; FAT: 7G; SATURATED FAT: 1G; CHOLESTEROL: 98MG; CARBOHYDRATES: 5G; FIBER: 2G; PROTEIN: 36G; SODIUM: 875MG

Tex-Mex Sweet Potato Skillet with Chicken

SERVES 4 TO 6 • PREP TIME: 15 MINUTES • COOK TIME: 20 MINUTES

I first had this dish on a camping trip, where we cooked it over a fire, and it was delicious. This version is full of everything I love in a Tex-Mex dish: black beans, corn, and, of course, the star of the dish, sweet potatoes. Serve with a side salad.

2 tablespoons extra-virgin olive oil

3 large sweet potatoes (1½ pounds), diced

1 pound boneless, skinless chicken breasts, cut into 1-inch pieces

1 onion, chopped

2 large garlic cloves, minced

2 large red bell peppers, diced

1 (15-ounce) can low-sodium black beans, rinsed and drained

1 cup frozen corn

2 tablespoons taco seasoning

1 cup shredded low-fat Cheddar cheese

1 avocado, pitted, peeled, and diced (optional)

1. In a large skillet over medium-high, heat the olive oil until hot.

2. Add the sweet potatoes and chicken. Cook for about 6 minutes, or until the chicken is browned and cooked through.

3. Add the onion, garlic, and bell peppers and cook for 3 minutes more, or until the sweet potatoes are tender.

4. Stir in the black beans, corn, and taco seasoning to combine. Cook for about 5 minutes, or until everything is heated through.

5. Garnish with the Cheddar cheese and avocado (if using) and serve. Refrigerate leftovers in an airtight container for up to 4 days.

VARIATION TIP: Make a double batch of this recipe and serve it in the morning with a fried or poached egg on top. You can also substitute turkey, ham, or even tofu for the chicken or omit the protein completely for a vegetarian dish.

PER SERVING: CALORIES: 579; FAT: 15G; SATURATED FAT: 5G; CHOLESTEROL: 80MG; CARBOHYDRATES: 72G; FIBER: 13G; PROTEIN: 41G; SODIUM: 743MG

Tuscan Chicken with Vegetables

SERVES 4 TO 6 • PREP TIME: 15 MINUTES • COOK TIME: 25 MINUTES

Chicken and vegetables is one of my go-to recipes and is often on our meal plan. I use zucchini here, but use any summer vegetables you want.

2 tablespoons extra-virgin olive oil, divided

1½ pounds boneless, skinless chicken breasts

2 tablespoons Italian seasoning

2 zucchini, cut into rounds

4 garlic cloves, minced

12 ounces green beans, trimmed

½ teaspoon red pepper flakes

2 tablespoons white wine or low-sodium chicken broth

1 cup grape tomatoes, halved

½ cup grated Parmesan cheese (optional)

1. In a large skillet over medium-high, heat 1 tablespoon of olive oil until hot.

2. Season both sides of the chicken with the Italian seasoning and add it to the skillet. Cook for about 6 minutes per side, depending on thickness, or until the chicken is done and the juices run clear. Remove the chicken from the skillet and keep warm.

3. Return the skillet to the heat and add the remaining 1 tablespoon of olive oil to heat.

4. Add the zucchini, garlic, and green beans. Sauté for about 4 minutes, allowing the vegetables to soften.

5. Stir in the red pepper flakes, white wine, and tomatoes. Cook for about 4 minutes, or until the tomatoes are heated through.

6. Sprinkle with the Parmesan cheese (if using). Refrigerate leftovers in an airtight container for up to 3 days.

INGREDIENT TIP: To make your own Tuscan seasoning, simply combine 2 tablespoons crushed rosemary, 1 table-spoon dried basil, 1 tablespoon dried thyme, 2 teaspoons onion powder, 2 teaspoons garlic powder, 1 teaspoon marjoram, 1 teaspoon crushed fennel seeds, and ½ tea-spoon salt in a small jar. Store extra in an airtight container for up to a year.

PER SERVING: CALORIES: 290; FAT: 11G; SATURATED FAT: 2G; CHOLESTEROL: 98MG; CARBOHYDRATES: 14G; FIBER: 5G; PROTEIN: 38G; SODIUM: 291MG

Egg Roll in a Bowl

SERVES 4 • PREP TIME: 10 MINUTES • COOK TIME: 20 MINUTES

I first had egg roll in a bowl while following a low-carb diet. My husband loves egg rolls, and this recipe gave us what we were craving. Add some wonton chips for a little crunch.

1 tablespoon sesame oil

1 onion, diced

1½ pounds ground turkey or ground pork

5 garlic cloves, minced

1 teaspoon ground ginger

¼ cup low-sodium soy sauce

1 (1-pound) bag coleslaw mix

1 cup shredded carrots

Salt

Freshly ground black pepper

½ cup sliced scallion

1. In a large skillet over medium-high, heat the sesame oil.

2. Add the onion and cook for about 6 minutes, or until it softens.

3. Add the ground turkey and cook for about 6 minutes, stirring to break up the meat, or until cooked and no longer pink.

4. Stir in the garlic, ginger, soy sauce, coleslaw mix, and carrots. Cover the skillet and cook for about 7 minutes, or until the cabbage wilts.

5. Taste and season with salt and pepper. Serve garnished with the scallion.

SUBSTITUTION TIP: Make this dish gluten-free by substituting coconut aminos or tamari for the soy sauce.

PER SERVING: CALORIES: 344; FAT: 16G; SATURATED FAT: 4G; CHOLESTEROL: 120MG; CARBOHYDRATES: 15G; FIBER: 2G; PROTEIN: 36G; SODIUM: 725MG

Pork Chops with Collard Greens

SERVES 4 • PREP TIME: 20 MINUTES • COOK TIME: 40 MINUTES

Collard greens are a great source of protein (surprise!), as well as calcium and potassium. I love cooking them in the same skillet as my pork chops because they pick up a little of that salty, smoky flavor from the pan. Do yourself a favor and look for prewashed and precut bags of collard greens at the grocery store, which will save a lot of prep time.

3 tablespoons extra-virgin olive oil, divided

4 (1-inch-thick) bone-in pork chops

2 tablespoons low-sodium Montreal steak seasoning or seasoning of your choice

2 small onions, diced

2 (1-pound) packages collard greens or 2 bunches greens, chopped

4 garlic cloves, minced

1. In a large skillet over medium, heat 1 tablespoon of olive oil until hot.

2. Season both sides of the pork chops with the Montreal steak seasoning. Working in batches, add 2 chops to the skillet. Cook for 6 minutes, flip, and cook for 6 to 7 minutes more, or until they reach an internal temperature of 145°F. Transfer the chops to serving plates to rest, and cover with foil to keep warm. Repeat with the remaining 2 pork chops and 1 tablespoon of olive oil. Remove from the skillet and keep warm.

3. In the same skillet, heat the remaining 1 tablespoon of olive oil until hot.

4. Add the onions and cook for about 2 minutes, or until they just start to soften.

5. Add the collard greens and garlic. Stir, cover the skillet, and cook for 6 to 7 minutes, or until tender. Serve with the pork.

LOVE YOUR LEFTOVERS: Keep leftover collard greens in the refrigerator; they are great the next morning in a breakfast burrito or a quiche.

PER SERVING: CALORIES: 330; FAT: 25G; SATURATED FAT: 4G; CHOLESTEROL: 57MG; CARBOHYDRATES: 12G; FIBER: 4G; PROTEIN: 20G; SODIUM: 2,410MG

American Goulash

SERVES 6 • PREP TIME: 10 MINUTES • COOK TIME: 35 MINUTES

American goulash is an easy, family-friendly meal that is full of flavor. Made with ground beef, paprika, tomatoes, and macaroni, this recipe will win over your kids any day of the week. This lighter version uses whole-wheat pasta and lots of tomatoes.

2 tablespoons extra-virgin olive oil

1 onion, chopped

2 garlic cloves, minced

1 pound extra-lean ground beef

1½ tablespoons tomato paste

1¼ cups low-sodium beef broth

1 (14-ounce) can tomato sauce

1 (14-ounce) can Italian-style diced tomatoes

1½ teaspoons paprika

1½ cups whole-wheat elbow macaroni

1 cup shredded low-fat Cheddar cheese (optional, but the sauce will not be as thick without the cheese)

1. In a large skillet over medium, heat the olive oil until hot.

2. Add the onion and sauté for 5 minutes. Stir in the garlic.

3. Add the ground beef to the skillet and cook for 6 to 8 minutes, stirring to break up the meat, or until cooked through and no longer pink. Drain if needed.

4. Stir in the tomato paste to coat the beef mixture.

5. Add the beef broth, tomato sauce, tomatoes, paprika, and macaroni. Stir to combine. Bring the goulash to a simmer, stirring occasionally. Cook for about 15 minutes, or until the macaroni is cooked through.

6. Turn off the heat and fold in the Cheddar cheese (if using).

LOVE YOUR LEFTOVERS: The best part of this recipe is the leftovers. Refrigerate leftovers in an airtight container for up to 5 days. I like to reheat them in the microwave for a quick lunch. You can also serve the leftovers on a whole-wheat bun for a quick, sloppy Joe–like sandwich.

PER SERVING: CALORIES: 294; FAT: 8G; SATURATED FAT: 2G; CHOLESTEROL: 44MG; CARBOHYDRATES: 33G; FIBER: 6G; PROTEIN: 23G; SODIUM: 559MG

CHINESE CHICKEN SALAD, PAGE 117

CHAPTER SIX

Double-Duty Dinners

Roasted Portobello Mushrooms with Confetti Corn

SERVES 4 • PREP TIME: 20 MINUTES • COOK TIME: 25 MINUTES

You can serve this recipe to your vegetarian friends and your meat-loving friends, and everyone will enjoy it. I pair these portobello mushrooms with one of my favorite side dishes of all time, confetti corn. A big green salad makes this recipe a complete meal. Use the extra mushrooms to make the Portobello & Black Bean Burgers on page 102.

⅓ cup low-sodium soy sauce

3 tablespoons balsamic vinegar

5 garlic cloves, minced

4 tablespoons extra-virgin olive oil, divided

6 large portobello mushroom caps

4 cups fresh or frozen and thawed corn

1 large red bell pepper, diced

¼ teaspoon cayenne pepper

Pinch salt

¼ cup chopped fresh cilantro

1. Preheat the oven to 400°F. Line a sheet pan with aluminum foil. Set aside.

2. In a large bowl, whisk the soy sauce, vinegar, garlic, and 2 tablespoons of olive oil to blend.

3. Place the mushroom caps, stem-side down, on the prepared sheet pan. Pour the sauce over the mushrooms and rub it in to ensure they are fully covered. Let the mushrooms sit for 15 minutes. Baste the mushrooms again with any leftover sauce.

4. Roast for 10 minutes. Turn the mushrooms over and roast for 10 to 15 minutes more, depending on their size, or until they are deep brown. Remove and set aside.

5. While the mushrooms cook, in a large skillet over high, heat the remaining 2 tablespoons of olive oil until hot.

6. Stir in the corn, bell pepper, cayenne, and salt. Cook for 10 to 15 minutes, stirring occasionally, or until the bell pepper is tender. Sprinkle with the cilantro and keep warm.

7. Reserve 2 mushrooms for **Portobello & Black Bean Burgers** (page 102), if desired, refrigerated in an airtight container for up to 4 days.

8. Slice the remaining mushrooms and serve with the corn.

COOKING TIP: If the weather is nice, this is an excellent recipe to cook on the grill. Marinate the mushroom caps for about 15 minutes. Preheat the grill to medium-high heat. Grill the mushroom for 4 to 5 minutes per side, or until a deep brown color. You can even put a grill-safe pan directly on the grates and make the confetti corn right there at the same time.

PER SERVING: CALORIES 302; FAT: 16G; SATURATED FAT: 2G; CHOLESTEROL: 0MG; CARBOHYDRATES: 39G; FIBER: 6G; PROTEIN: 9G; SODIUM: 556MG

Portobello & Black Bean Burgers

SERVES 4 • PREP TIME: 15 MINUTES • COOK TIME: 10 MINUTES

These burgers are so much better than the black bean burgers you get in the freezer aisle at the grocery store. Whereas those can be dry and cardboard-like, these have great flavor. If the mixture starts to fall apart when you shape the patties, add a little more bread crumbs.

1 (15-ounce) can low-sodium black beans, rinsed and drained

2 cooked portobello mushroom caps from **Roasted Portobello Mushrooms with Confetti Corn (page 100)**, finely chopped

1 cup finely chopped broccoli

1 carrot, finely chopped

2 large eggs

¼ cup shredded part-skim mozzarella cheese

3 tablespoons rolled oats or panko bread crumbs

2 tablespoons steak sauce

1 tablespoon Montreal steak seasoning

2 tablespoons extra-virgin olive oil

1. In a medium bowl, mash the black beans with a fork until they are mostly smooth.

2. Stir in the mushrooms, broccoli, and carrot.

3. Add the eggs, mozzarella cheese, oats, steak sauce, and steak seasoning and mix well to combine. Form the bean mixture into 4 patties, using about ½ cup of mixture for each.

4. In a skillet over medium-high, heat the olive oil until hot. Add the patties to the skillet and cook for 5 minutes per side, or until golden brown.

SERVING TIP: My kids like cheese, so I put a slice of Cheddar cheese on their burgers right before they finish cooking. I prefer mine without a bun, but you can serve these just like regular hamburgers.

PER SERVING: CALORIES: 284; FAT: 13G; SATURATED FAT: 3G; CHOLESTEROL: 97MG; CARBOHYDRATES: 28G; FIBER: 7G; PROTEIN: 14G; SODIUM: 1,007MG

Grilled Eggplant and Polenta with Apple Slaw

SERVES 4 • PREP TIME: 15 MINUTES, PLUS 30 MINUTES TO SALT THE EGGPLANT
COOK TIME: 15 MINUTES

In summer, I love to grill whenever I have the chance, and eggplant is great for grilling. The trick is to draw out the moisture by salting the eggplant before you grill it, so don't skip this step. Save the extra eggplant for the Eggplant & Tomato Pitas with Tzatziki on page 105.

3 eggplants, cut into ½-inch rounds

3 tablespoons coarse salt, plus more for seasoning

½ cup extra-virgin olive oil, plus 1 tablespoon

2 garlic cloves, minced

Freshly ground black pepper

2 to 3 tablespoons finely chopped fresh parsley (optional)

1 (18-ounce) roll polenta, cut into ¾-inch-thick rounds

1 (1-pound) bag coleslaw mix

1 apple, cored and thinly sliced

½ cup Maple Mustard Vinaigrette (page 34)

½ cup raisins or dried cranberries (optional)

1. Sprinkle the eggplant slices on both sides with the salt. Let sit for 30 minutes. This will remove the water and some of the bitterness. Rinse the eggplants and pat dry with paper towels. Place the eggplant slices on a sheet pan.

2. Preheat the grill or a grill pan to medium-high heat.

3. In a small bowl, whisk ½ cup of olive oil and the garlic to combine. Using a pastry brush, brush the olive oil and garlic mixture on both sides of the eggplant slices. Season with salt, pepper, and the parsley (if using).

4. Place the eggplant slices on the grill and cook for 6 to 7 minutes per side, or until soft and golden brown. Reserve 1½ cups of eggplant slices, refrigerated in an airtight container for up to 4 days, for **Eggplant & Tomato Pitas with Tzatziki** (page 105).

5. Using a pastry brush and the remaining 1 tablespoon of olive oil, brush each polenta round on both sides. Place the slices on the grill and cook for 7 to 8 minutes per side, or until golden brown.

CONTINUED

6. While the eggplants and polenta cook, make the apple slaw. In a large bowl, combine the coleslaw mix and apple. Pour in the vinaigrette and sprinkle in the raisins (if using). Toss well to coat. Serve with the grilled eggplant and polenta.

LOVE YOUR LEFTOVERS: When reserving leftovers for another meal, it's important to handle them safely to prevent unwelcome bacteria from growing. Be sure to cover and refrigerate them within 2 hours of cooking.

PER SERVING: CALORIES: 503; FAT: 33G; SATURATED FAT: 5G; CHOLESTEROL: 0MG; CARBOHYDRATES: 50G; FIBER: 11G; PROTEIN: 7G; SODIUM: 1,223MG

Eggplant & Tomato Pitas with Tzatziki

SERVES 4 • PREP TIME: 15 MINUTES, PLUS 1 HOUR CHILLING • COOK TIME: 20 MINUTES

Eggplant paired with tzatziki is a delicious combination, and this recipe is perfect for meatless Mondays. Reheating eggplant in the oven takes about 20 minutes and the tzatziki needs a good hour in the refrigerator for the flavors to meld, so plan accordingly.

1 cup low-fat plain Greek yogurt

1 small cucumber, seeded and chopped

1 tablespoon freshly squeezed lemon juice

1 teaspoon garlic powder

1 teaspoon chopped fresh dill

1½ cups grilled eggplant from **Grilled Eggplant and Polenta with Apple Slaw** (page 103), diced

1 cup grape tomatoes or cherry tomatoes, halved

1½ cups canned low-sodium chickpeas, rinsed and drained

¼ cup chopped fresh parsley

4 whole-wheat pita pockets, halved

2 romaine lettuce leaves, thinly sliced

1. In a food processor or blender, combine the yogurt, cucumber, lemon juice, garlic powder, and dill. Process until smooth. Place in a covered container and refrigerate for at least 1 hour. You can make the tzatziki up to 3 days in advance.

2. Preheat the oven to 350°F.

3. Place the eggplant in an oven-safe dish and warm in oven for 10 minutes.

4. Stir in the tomatoes, chickpeas, and parsley. Bake for 10 minutes more.

5. Assemble the pitas by placing the eggplant mixture in the pita halves, followed by the lettuce and tzatziki.

LOVE YOUR LEFTOVERS: This tzatziki sauce is so good you are going to want to make extra. You can use it as a raw veggie dip, and it also pairs nicely with fish.

PER SERVING: CALORIES: 382; FAT: 10G; SATURATED FAT: 2G; CHOLESTEROL: 9MG; CARBOHYDRATES: 60G; FIBER: 13G; PROTEIN: 19G; SODIUM: 779MG

Sheet Pan Blackened Tilapia with Broccoli & Carrots

SERVES 4 • PREP TIME: 10 MINUTES • COOK TIME: 15 MINUTES

Every time I make tilapia, I ask myself why I don't cook it more often. I like a mild fish, and tilapia fits the bill. It takes on a lot of the flavor of the seasoning you use, so don't be shy. Leftovers are great in the Easy Tilapia Fish Cakes with Mixed Greens (page 108), so don't eat it all in one go.

3 tablespoons paprika

1 tablespoon dried parsley flakes

2 teaspoons salt

2 teaspoons onion powder

2 teaspoons garlic powder

1 teaspoon freshly ground black pepper

½ teaspoon cayenne pepper

2 cups broccoli florets

1½ cups sliced carrots

2 tablespoons extra-virgin olive oil, divided

6 tilapia fillets

1. Preheat the oven to 400°F. Line a sheet pan with a silicone baking mat or aluminum foil. Set aside.

2. In a small bowl, whisk the paprika, parsley, salt, onion powder, garlic powder, black pepper, and cayenne pepper to combine.

3. Place the broccoli and carrots on the prepared sheet pan. Drizzle with 1 tablespoon of olive oil and a pinch of spice mixture. Using your hands, toss the vegetables to coat. Push the vegetables to the sides of the pan.

4. Pat dry the tilapia fillets with paper towels. Using a pastry brush, brush the fillets on both sides with the remaining 1 tablespoon of olive oil. Generously season each side with the spice mixture. Place the fillets in the middle of the sheet pan.

5. Bake for 13 to 15 minutes, or until the fillets are opaque and flake easily with a fork.

6. Reserve 2 cooked fillets, refrigerated in an airtight container for up to 2 days, for **Easy Tilapia Fish Cakes with Mixed Greens** (page 108).

7. Serve the remaining tilapia with the vegetables on the side.

INGREDIENT TIP: You can use frozen tilapia, but I recommend thawing it before baking. Place the frozen fillets in the refrigerator overnight. If you forget, seal the fillets in a gallon-size resealable bag and submerge in cold water for about 1 hour.

PER SERVING: CALORIES: 215; FAT: 8G; SATURATED FAT: 2G; CHOLESTEROL: 58MG; CARBOHYDRATES: 11G; FIBER: 4G; PROTEIN: 25G; SODIUM: 1,268MG

Easy Tilapia Fish Cakes with Mixed Greens

SERVES 2 • PREP TIME: 15 MINUTES, PLUS 1 HOUR CHILLING • COOK TIME: 15 MINUTES

We have these fish cakes frequently. They are a nice and easy way to enjoy leftover seafood in a slightly less traditional way. You could even add some extra spice with sriracha, if it suits you.

2 cooked tilapia fillets from **Sheet Pan Blackened Tilapia with Broccoli & Carrots** (page 106)

¼ cup low-fat plain Greek yogurt

1 large egg, beaten

2 tablespoons chopped fresh chives

1 tablespoon chopped fresh oregano leaves

2 teaspoons Dijon mustard

½ cup panko bread crumbs

2 tablespoons extra-virgin olive oil

4 cups mixed salad greens

¼ cup store-bought balsamic vinaigrette

1. In a large bowl, using 2 forks, shred the tilapia.

2. Add the yogurt, egg, chives, oregano, mustard, and bread crumbs. Mix well. Form the tilapia mixture into 4 or 5 (1-inch-thick) patties. Cover the patties and refrigerate for 1 hour.

3. In a nonstick skillet over medium-high, heat the olive oil until hot. Add the tilapia cakes and cook for 5 to 6 minutes per side, or until browned.

4. In another large bowl, combine the mixed greens and vinaigrette. Toss to coat and serve with the fish cakes.

VARIATION TIP: These fish cakes are delicious topped with a dollop of low-fat plain Greek yogurt or with a side of tzatziki (page 105).

PER SERVING: CALORIES: 507; FAT: 28G; SATURATED FAT: 4G; CHOLESTEROL: 155MG; CARBOHYDRATES: 32G; FIBER: 5G; PROTEIN: 35G; SODIUM: 1,180MG

Sheet Pan Chicken & Asparagus

SERVES 4 • PREP TIME: 15 MINUTES • COOK TIME: 30 MINUTES

There is a nice sweetness from the honey, which gives this chicken the perfect flavor and balances with the lemon and herbs. It makes for a nice summery meal throughout the year.

3 tablespoons extra-virgin olive oil

3 tablespoons honey

3 garlic cloves, minced

1 tablespoon herbes de Provence

Zest and juice of 1 lemon

6 boneless, skinless chicken breasts

Salt

Freshly ground black pepper

1 lemon, thinly sliced into thin rounds

2½ pounds asparagus, woody ends trimmed

Chopped fresh flat-leaf parsley, for garnish (optional)

1. Preheat the oven to 400°F. Line a baking sheet with aluminum foil. Set aside.

2. In a small bowl, whisk the olive oil, honey, garlic, herbes de Provence, and lemon zest and juice until well combined.

3. Season the chicken breasts all over with salt and pepper. Place the chicken on the prepared sheet pan and pour half the sauce over the chicken. Top the chicken with the lemon rounds. Cover the pan with aluminum foil.

4. Bake for 20 minutes. Place the asparagus around the chicken. Pour the remaining sauce over the asparagus.

5. Turn the oven to broil.

6. Broil the chicken and asparagus for about 10 minutes, or until the chicken is browned and reaches an internal temperature of at least 165°F.

7. Reserve 2 cooked chicken breasts and about 10 cooked asparagus spears, refrigerated in an airtight container for up to 3 days, for **Chicken & Asparagus Omelet with Tomato Salad** (page 110).

8. Sprinkle the remaining chicken and asparagus with parsley (if using) and serve. Refrigerate leftovers in an airtight container for up to 3 days.

PER SERVING: CALORIES: 252; FAT: 10G; SATURATED FAT: 2G; CHOLESTEROL: 65MG; CARBOHYDRATES: 19G; FIBER: 4G; PROTEIN: 28G; SODIUM: 185MG

Chicken & Asparagus Omelet with Tomato Salad

SERVES 2 • PREP TIME: 15 MINUTES • COOK TIME: 30 MINUTES

This is a great recipe to bookmark because you can use up a lot of leftovers making omelets. Once you master the method, the sky's the limit. Just change the protein and the cheese for an entirely different meal; you'll need about 1 cup of filling per omelet.

1 teaspoon salt, divided

½ teaspoon freshly ground black pepper, divided

1 tablespoon extra-virgin olive oil

1 tablespoon balsamic vinegar

1 pint grape tomatoes, halved

2 cooked chicken breasts from **Sheet Pan Chicken & Asparagus** (page 109), cut into bite-size pieces

10 cooked asparagus spears from **Sheet Pan Chicken & Asparagus** (page 109), cut into bite-size pieces

6 large eggs

3 teaspoons butter, divided

4 tablespoons shredded low-fat Cheddar cheese or any cheese you like, divided

1 tablespoon chopped fresh parsley

1. In a medium bowl, whisk ½ teaspoon of salt, ¼ teaspoon of pepper, the olive oil, and vinegar until combined. Add the tomatoes and stir well to combine. Set aside.

2. In an 8-inch skillet over medium-low, combine the chicken and asparagus. Cook for about 4 minutes, stirring occasionally, or until heated through. Remove from the skillet and reserve.

3. In a medium bowl, whisk the eggs, remaining ½ teaspoon of salt, and ¼ teaspoon of pepper until well beaten.

4. Return the skillet to the stovetop and increase the heat to medium. Melt 1½ teaspoons of butter. Add half the egg mixture and cook for about 4 minutes, or until the sides of the eggs start to set. Using a rubber spatula, push the eggs to the middle of the skillet so the uncooked egg mixture flows to the edges and cooks. Cook for 1 to 2 minutes, or until the eggs are mostly set.

5. Add half the chicken mixture to one side of the omelet and sprinkle with 2 tablespoons of Cheddar cheese. Using a spatula, fold the empty side of the omelet over the filling. Cook for about 3 minutes, or until the cheese starts to melt. Remove the omelet from the pan and garnish with ½ tablespoon of parsley. Cover to keep warm. Repeat to make a second omelet.

6. Serve with the tomato salad.

COOKING TIP: Make the tomato salad the night before and refrigerate overnight. The tomatoes will pick up a lot of flavor from the vinegar. You could also add some basil or small mozzarella balls to the salad, if you like.

PER SERVING: CALORIES: 624; FAT: 39G; SATURATED FAT: 12G; CHOLESTEROL: 644MG; CARBOHYDRATES: 25G; FIBER: 4G; PROTEIN: 48G; SODIUM: 1,688MG

Sheet Pan Chicken Fajitas

SERVES 4 TO 6 • PREP TIME: 15 MINUTES, PLUS 1 HOUR MARINATING
COOK TIME: 20 MINUTES

This recipe is the reason I fell in love with sheet pan meals. We have a pretty busy life with our young kids, and this meal has been a huge time-saver for my family. I always make a double batch and keep the leftovers in the refrigerator for lunches because it's great in so many recipes. This recipe makes enough for either the Easy Chicken Fajita Salad (page 113) or Chicken Fajita Pizza (page 114).

½ cup or 2 (1.12-ounce) packets fajita seasoning

3 garlic cloves, minced

2 tablespoons extra-virgin olive oil

Juice of 1 lime

2½ pounds boneless, skinless chicken breasts, cut into ½-inch-thick strips

4 bell peppers, any color, cut into strips

1 onion, thinly sliced

Nonstick cooking spray, for coating

¼ cup chopped fresh cilantro

8 to 10 (8-inch) flour tortillas, warmed

1 lime, cut into wedges

Low-fat plain Greek yogurt, for topping

Diced avocado, for topping

Salsa, for topping

Shredded cheese of choice, for topping

1. In a large bowl, whisk the fajita seasoning, garlic, olive oil, and lime juice until well combined. Add the chicken, bell peppers, and onion. Stir until coated. Cover the bowl with plastic wrap and refrigerate for 1 to 2 hours.

2. Preheat the oven to 400°F. Spray a sheet pan with cooking spray or line it with a silicone liner.

3. Spread the chicken and vegetables in an even layer on the prepared sheet pan.

4. Roast for 15 to 20 minutes, or until the peppers are soft and the chicken reaches an internal temperature of 165°F.

5. Reserve 2 cups of cooked chicken and vegetable mixture, refrigerated in an airtight container for up to 4 days, for **Easy Chicken Fajita Salad** (page 113) or **Chicken Fajita Pizza** (page 114).

6. Serve the remaining chicken fajitas with the tortillas, lime wedges, and toppings of choice.

COOKING TIP: When slicing any kind of meat, be sure to cut against the grain. This ensures the chicken won't be chewy.

PER SERVING: CALORIES: 647; FAT: 16G; SATURATED FAT: 3G; CHOLESTEROL: 114MG; CARBOHYDRATES: 71G; FIBER: 6G; PROTEIN: 50G; SODIUM: 1,949MG

Easy Chicken Fajita Salad

SERVES 4 • PREP TIME: 10 MINUTES • COOK TIME: 3 MINUTES (OPTIONAL)

This is a great recipe to bring to work for lunch. You can make a large batch of chicken during meal prep and make a few salads for the week. Add the dressing when you're ready to eat. You can also make a big batch of dressing and refrigerate it in a tightly lidded jar for up to 1 week.

1 romaine lettuce heart, chopped

1 cup grape tomatoes, quartered

¾ cup Zesty Lime Dressing (page 34), divided

2 cups cooked chicken and vegetables from **Sheet Pan Chicken Fajitas** (page 112), warmed, if desired (see tip)

¼ cup shredded low-fat Cheddar cheese (optional)

1 cup crushed tortilla chips (optional)

1. In a serving bowl, toss together the lettuce and tomatoes. Add ½ cup of dressing and toss to coat. Serve the remaining ¼ cup of dressing on the side.

2. Place the chicken fajitas on top of the salad and sprinkle with the Cheddar cheese (if using) and tortilla chips (if using).

SERVING TIP: I like my chicken chilled on salads, but feel free to warm it if you like. In a microwave-safe bowl, heat the chicken on 80 percent power for 2 to 3 minutes.

PER SERVING: CALORIES: 327; FAT: 23G; SATURATED FAT: 3G; CHOLESTEROL: 49MG: CARBOHYDRATES: 10G; FIBER: 1G; PROTEIN: 18G; SODIUM: 721MG

Chicken Fajita Pizza

SERVES 6 • PREP TIME: 15 MINUTES • COOK TIME: 20 MINUTES

Pizza can be good for you. This version uses a whole-wheat crust topped with loads of great vegetables and leftovers from Sheet Pan Chicken Fajitas (page 112) and includes healthy fats from the avocado.

Whole-wheat flour, for dusting

1 pound whole-wheat pizza dough (store-bought is perfect)

1 tablespoon extra-virgin olive oil

2 cups cooked chicken fajitas from **Sheet Pan Chicken Fajitas (page 112)**, diced

8 ounces shredded Colby-Jack cheese

1 avocado, peeled, pitted, and diced

¼ cup chopped fresh cilantro

1. Preheat the oven to 450°F.
2. Dust a work surface with flour and place the dough on it. Roll out the dough into a large pizza shape, about ½ inch thick, and place it on a baking sheet. Using a pastry brush, brush the dough with the olive oil.
3. Top with the chicken fajitas and vegetables. Sprinkle the Colby-Jack cheese over the entire pizza.
4. Bake for 15 to 20 minutes, or until the pizza crust is golden brown and cooked.
5. Top with the avocado and cilantro and serve.

VARIATION TIP: Use this recipe with any variety of pre-made flatbread. Top two flatbreads with the chicken and vegetable mixture and cheese. Bake for about 8 minutes, or until the cheese is melted. If you enjoy sauce on your pizza, add a few tablespoons of barbecue sauce before topping and omit the olive oil.

PER SERVING: CALORIES: 487; FAT: 24G; SATURATED FAT: 8G; CHOLESTEROL: 73MG; CARBOHYDRATES: 41G; FIBER: 3G; PROTEIN: 27G; SODIUM: 974MG

Healthier Orange Chicken

SERVES 4 TO 6 • PREP TIME: 15 MINUTES • COOK TIME: 15 MINUTES

When that craving for deep-fried Chinese takeout hits, make a healthier version at home instead. This recipe doesn't take long and tastes better than anything you order. The chicken isn't deep-fried or coated in any kind of batter, so the leftovers are great to use in other recipes. This recipe makes enough leftovers to make the Easy Chicken Lettuce Wraps (page 116) or the Chinese Chicken Salad (page 117).

2 tablespoons extra-virgin olive oil

3 pounds boneless, skinless chicken breasts, diced

Salt

Freshly ground black pepper

Zest of 1 orange

Juice of 3 oranges (about 1 cup)

½ cup low-sodium soy sauce

⅓ cup honey

¼ cup apple cider vinegar

1½ tablespoons cornstarch

3 garlic cloves, minced

1 teaspoon grated peeled fresh ginger

1 scallion, sliced (optional)

Steamed broccoli, for serving

Cooked rice, for serving (optional)

1. In a skillet over medium-high, heat the olive oil until hot.

2. Season the chicken with salt and pepper and add it to the skillet. Cook for 6 to 8 minutes, stirring occasionally, or until browned on all sides.

3. In a small bowl, whisk the orange zest, orange juice, soy sauce, honey, vinegar, cornstarch, garlic, and ginger until smooth and combined. Reduce the heat to medium-low and stir the sauce into the chicken. Cook for 6 to 7 minutes, or until the sauce thickens and chicken is cooked through.

4. Reserve half the cooked orange chicken (4 cups), refrigerated in an airtight container for up to 4 days, for **Easy Chicken Lettuce Wraps** (page 116) or **Chinese Chicken Salad** (page 117).

5. Top the remaining chicken with the scallion (if using). Serve with broccoli and rice (if using) on the side.

SUBSTITUTION TIP: If you don't have fresh ginger, substitute ½ teaspoon ground ginger.

PER SERVING: CALORIES: 253; FAT: 7G; SATURATED FAT: 1G; CHOLESTEROL: 98MG; CARBOHYDRATES: 13G; FIBER: <1G; PROTEIN: 36G; SODIUM: 846MG

Easy Chicken Lettuce Wraps

SERVES: 4 TO 6 • PREP TIME: 10 MINUTES • COOK TIME: 5 MINUTES

This is my favorite way to use leftover Healthier Orange Chicken (page 115). I love making these wraps for lunch the next day, as the meat reheats well (although you can also serve the chicken cold), and I love the crunch from all the raw vegetables. They also work really well in lunch boxes.

4 cups cooked orange chicken from **Healthier Orange Chicken** (page 115)

2 cups coleslaw mix

2 tablespoons store-bought sesame dressing

8 to 10 Bibb lettuce leaves or green leaf or romaine lettuce leaves

1 scallion, sliced (optional)

1 teaspoon sesame seeds (optional)

1. Place the orange chicken in a large microwave-safe bowl and cover with a moist paper towel. Warm the chicken in the microwave for about 3 minutes, or until hot.

2. While the chicken heats, in a medium bowl, stir together the coleslaw mix and sesame dressing.

3. Divide the coleslaw and orange chicken among the lettuce leaves. Sprinkle with the scallion (if using) and sesame seeds (if using).

VARIATION TIP: For another sauce option for these lettuce wraps—with a little extra kick—try the garlic-chile sauce from the Fresh Veggie Spring Rolls with Garlic-Chile Sauce (page 58).

PER SERVING: CALORIES: 294; FAT: 11G; SATURATED FAT: 2G; CHOLESTEROL: 98MG; CARBOHYDRATES: 15G; FIBER: 1G; PROTEIN: 37G; SODIUM: 931MG

Chinese Chicken Salad

SERVES 4 • PREP TIME: 15 MINUTES • COOK TIME: 5 MINUTES

This retro salad is a great way to use up leftovers in your refrigerator. My husband and I eat salads several days a week, and my kids enjoy them, too. If you have enough orange chicken sauce in your leftover orange chicken from Healthier Orange Chicken (page 115), skip the sesame dressing.

4 cups cooked orange chicken from **Healthier Orange Chicken** (page 115)

4 cups chopped romaine lettuce

2 cups shredded red cabbage

1 cup julienned carrots

1 (8-ounce) can sliced water chestnuts

1 cup canned mandarin oranges, drained

½ cup store-bought sesame dressing

½ cup toasted pecans (optional)

1. If you prefer, place the orange chicken in a large microwave-safe bowl and cover with a moist paper towel. Warm the chicken in the microwave for about 3 minutes, or until hot. Alternatively, use the chicken cold.

2. In a large bowl, combine the romaine, red cabbage, carrots, water chestnuts, oranges, and sesame dressing. Toss to mix and coat the vegetables in the dressing.

3. Top with the orange chicken and sprinkle with the pecans (if using).

SUBSTITUTION TIP: I love pecans with oranges, but if you or a loved one is allergic to tree nuts, use wonton strips or chow mein noodles for a little extra crunch.

PER SERVING: CALORIES: 478; FAT: 21G; SATURATED FAT: 3G; CHOLESTEROL: 98MG; CARBOHYDRATES: 37G; FIBER: 5G; PROTEIN: 39G; SODIUM: 1,195MG

Baked Pork Tenderloin with Potatoes & Green Beans

SERVES 4 TO 6 • PREP TIME: 15 MINUTES • COOK TIME: 40 MINUTES

When my grocery store has a buy-one-get-one-free sale on pork tenderloins, I stock up and make this baked tenderloin recipe. With the leftovers, you'll have enough to make the Pork Quesadillas (page 120) or Spicy Pork with Ramen Noodles (page 121), or even use the pork in the Use-It-All-Up Leftover Fried Rice (page 62).

Cooking spray (optional)

2 tablespoons Italian seasoning

2 teaspoons salt

2 teaspoons freshly ground black pepper

2 (1½- to 2-pound) pork tenderloins

3 tablespoons extra-virgin olive oil, divided

1 pound green beans, trimmed

1 pound baby potatoes, halved

1. Preheat the oven to 400°F. Line a sheet pan with a silicone baking sheet or mist it with cooking spray. Set aside.

2. In a small dish, stir together the Italian seasoning, salt, and pepper. Reserve 1 teaspoon of seasoning for the vegetables and rub the remaining seasoning over the tenderloins.

3. In a large skillet over medium-high, heat 1 tablespoon of olive oil until hot. Add the tenderloins to sear for about 4 minutes per side, or until a nice crust forms.

4. While the tenderloins cook, in a large bowl, combine the green beans and potatoes. Drizzle the vegetables with the remaining 2 tablespoons of olive oil and sprinkle with the reserved 1 teaspoon of seasoning. Pour the vegetables onto the prepared sheet pan.

5. Place the tenderloins in the middle of the sheet pan.

6. Bake for 25 to 30 minutes, or until the internal temperature of the pork reaches 140°F to 145°F. Remove and let rest for at least 10 minutes.

7. Reserve 1 cooked tenderloin, refrigerated in an airtight container for up to 5 days, for **Pork Quesadillas** (page 120) or **Spicy Pork with Ramen Noodles** (page 121).

8. Slice the remaining tenderloin and serve with the green beans and potatoes.

VARIATION TIP: You can season the pork tenderloins with all kinds of sauces and seasonings to make a completely new meal. I like to baste mine with a honey-Dijon sauce or teriyaki sauce before cooking.

PER SERVING: CALORIES: 387; FAT: 15G; SATURATED FAT: 3G; CHOLESTEROL: 68MG; CARBOHYDRATES: 28G; FIBER: 7G; PROTEIN: 40G; SODIUM: 740MG

Pork Quesadillas

SERVES 4 • PREP TIME: 10 MINUTES • COOK TIME: 20 MINUTES

I love queso fresco in my quesadillas. If you are not familiar with this Mexican cheese, it is very mild and light, and it is great in summer salads or paired with a heavier cheese in recipes. We love it sprinkled on our corn on the cob in summer.

1 cooked pork tenderloin from **Baked Pork Tenderloin with Potatoes & Green Beans** (page 118), diced (about 2 cups)

1 (15-ounce) can low-sodium black beans, rinsed and drained

½ cup fresh or frozen and thawed corn

½ cup salsa, plus more for serving

⅓ cup chopped fresh cilantro

4 (8-inch) whole-wheat tortillas

6 ounces shredded part-skim mozzarella cheese

4 tablespoons crumbled queso fresco

Low-fat plain Greek yogurt, for serving (optional)

1. In a medium bowl, stir together the pork, black beans, corn, salsa, and cilantro.

2. In a large nonstick skillet over medium, place 1 tortilla, spread half the pork mixture over the tortilla, and cover with 3 ounces of mozzarella cheese and 2 tablespoons of queso fresco. Place a second tortilla on top. Cook for about 4 minutes, or until the tortilla is golden brown. Carefully flip the quesadilla and cook for 3 minutes more, or until the cheese is melted. Cut into 4 wedges and repeat for a second quesadilla.

3. Serve with more salsa and Greek yogurt (if using) for topping.

COOKING TIP: If you find it difficult to flip the large quesadilla, spread the filling on just half the tortilla and fold the other half over the filling. I find this a lot easier to work with. Make 4 quesadillas instead of 2 with one-quarter of the pork for each.

PER SERVING: CALORIES: 607; FAT: 21G; SATURATED FAT: 9G; CHOLESTEROL: 94MG; CARBOHYDRATES: 49G; FIBER: 8G; PROTEIN: 59G; SODIUM: 1,532MG

Spicy Pork with Ramen Noodles

SERVES 6 • PREP TIME: 10 MINUTES • COOK TIME: 15 MINUTES

This recipe comes from my love of ramen, but with a much healthier twist. Throw away those seasoning packets and use real ingredients to give the noodles flavor. Ramen pairs so nicely with pork and this recipe doesn't take much more time to make than the instant ramen from my youth.

6 cups water

3 (3-oz) packages ramen noodles, seasoning packets discarded

⅓ cup low-sodium soy sauce

⅓ cup low-sodium chicken broth

¼ cup honey

2 tablespoons store-bought garlic-chile sauce or Garlic-Chile Sauce (page 58)

1 tablespoon extra-virgin olive oil

1 cooked pork tenderloin from **Baked Pork Tenderloin with Potatoes & Green Beans** (page 118), thinly sliced

1 cup julienned carrots

1 cup shredded cabbage

¼ cup sliced scallion

1. In a large saucepan over high, bring the water to a boil. Add the ramen noodles and cook for 3 to 4 minutes, or until tender. Drain the noodles and set aside.

2. While the noodles cook, in a small bowl, whisk the soy sauce, chicken broth, honey, and garlic-chile sauce to blend.

3. In a skillet over medium, heat the olive oil until hot.

4. Add the pork and cook for 1 minute. Add the sauce and stir to coat the pork.

5. Stir in the carrots and cabbage. Cover the skillet, reduce the heat to low, and cook for 5 to 6 minutes, until the cabbage is tender.

6. Add the noodles to the skillet and toss to coat and warm. Serve the noodles and pork in bowls, topped with the scallion.

VARIATION TIP: Use any protein or vegetables you have on hand in this recipe. To make your noodles more or less spicy, adjust the garlic-chile sauce to your liking.

PER SERVING: CALORIES: 505; FAT: 24G; SATURATED FAT: 7G; CHOLESTEROL: 89MG; CARBOHYDRATES: 41G; FIBER: 2G; PROTEIN: 39G; SODIUM: 622MG

Broiled Flank Steaks with Brussels Sprouts & Sweet Potatoes

SERVES 4 TO 6 • PREP TIME: 10 MINUTES • COOK TIME: 15 MINUTES

I used to be afraid of my broiler. When I was in my early twenties, I hardly ever used it, except to melt cheese on tortilla chips. Boy, was I missing out. Cooking foods at a very high temperature caramelizes the exterior and keeps the inside tender. Don't be intimidated like I was; instead, learn to love your broiler.

2 cups Brussels sprouts, halved

4 sweet potatoes, diced (3 cups)

1 tablespoon extra-virgin olive oil

1 tablespoon herbes de Provence

2 teaspoons salt

1½ teaspoons freshly ground black pepper

2 (1-pound) flank steaks, trimmed

1. Preheat the broiler, positioning an oven rack about 6 inches from the heat source. Line a sheet pan with aluminum foil. Set aside.

2. In a large bowl, combine the Brussels sprouts and sweet potatoes. Drizzle the olive oil over the vegetables and toss to coat. Pour the vegetables onto the prepared sheet pan.

3. In a small dish, stir together the herbes de Provence, salt, and pepper. Using half the seasoning, season one side of each flank steak and place them, seasoned-side up, on the prepared sheet pan.

4. Broil for 10 minutes. Turn the steaks over and season the other side with the remaining seasoning.

5. Broil until the vegetables are tender and browned and the steaks are cooked to your desired level of doneness, or about 5 minutes to reach 145°F for medium.

6. Remove the steaks from the oven and let rest for at least 5 minutes. Reserve 1 cooked steak, refrigerated in an airtight container for up to 4 days, for **Open-Face Steak Sandwiches** (page 124) or **Steak Buddha Bowl** (page 125). If making the Buddha bowl, also reserve 1 cup of cooked sweet potato, refrigerated in an airtight container for up to 4 days.

7. Slice the remaining steak against the grain and serve it with the sweet potatoes and Brussels sprouts on the side.

INGREDIENT TIP: Flank steak is traditionally a very tough cut of meat, so it benefits from a good marinade. Although you don't have to marinate the steak for this recipe, it will be even more delicious if you do. In a large bowl, whisk ½ cup extra-virgin olive oil, ⅓ cup red-wine vinegar, ¼ cup soy sauce, and 3 minced garlic cloves. Add the steaks and turn to coat. Cover the bowl and refrigerate to marinate for a couple hours before cooking.

PER SERVING: CALORIES: 327; FAT: 11G; SATURATED FAT: 1G; CHOLESTEROL: 45MG; CARBOHYDRATES: 29G; FIBER: 5G; PROTEIN: 27G; SODIUM: 671MG

Open-Face Steak Sandwiches

SERVES 4 • PREP TIME: 10 MINUTES • COOK TIME: 15 MINUTES

I grew up making steak sandwiches with leftover steak from the night before. My mom made such delicious French dip sandwiches that I still think about them today. This open-face version is a little more health conscious with its goat cheese and greens. Although you can use any bread you like (even two slices), I think one slice of sourdough is delicious—and plenty.

1 tablespoon extra-virgin olive oil

1 onion, sliced

1 green bell pepper, thinly sliced

1 cup sliced mushrooms

Salt

Freshly ground black pepper

1 cooked flank steak from **Broiled Flank Steaks with Brussels Sprouts & Sweet Potatoes** (page 122), thinly sliced against the grain

¼ cup soft goat cheese

1 tablespoon prepared horseradish, more or less as desired

4 thick sourdough bread slices, toasted if desired

½ cup fresh baby spinach or watercress

1. In a medium skillet over medium-high, heat the olive oil until hot.

2. Add the onion, bell pepper, and mushrooms. Sauté for 7 to 8 minutes, or until the mushrooms are golden and the vegetables are tender. Season with salt and black pepper. Remove the vegetables and set aside.

3. If you want the steak hot, place it in the skillet, return the skillet to the heat, and warm for about 4 minutes. Set aside.

4. In a small bowl, stir together the goat cheese and horseradish until well combined. Spread about 1 tablespoon of cheese mixture onto each slice of bread. Top with steak slices and then the vegetables. Top the vegetables with spinach. Halve the sandwiches to serve.

SUBSTITUTION TIP: If horseradish isn't your thing, substitute spicy brown mustard or leave it out completely (a good idea if you're serving kids).

PER SERVING: CALORIES: 451; FAT: 18G; SATURATED FAT: 3G; CHOLESTEROL: 48MG; CARBOHYDRATES: 39G; FIBER: 4G; PROTEIN: 32G; SODIUM: 1,076MG

Steak Buddha Bowl

SERVES 4 TO 6 • PREP TIME: 15 MINUTES • COOK TIME: 45 MINUTES

Are you familiar with Buddha bowls? If not, they're basically grain bowls with lots of interesting toppings, and you are going to love them. They are super easy to make, and you can customize them for every person in your family so there are no complaints during dinner.

1 cup uncooked pearled barley

1 cooked flank steak from **Broiled Flank Steaks with Brussels Sprouts & Sweet Potatoes** (page 122), thinly sliced against the grain

1 cup cooked sweet potato from **Broiled Flank Steaks with Brussels Sprouts & Sweet Potatoes** (page 122)

4 cups baby arugula

1 large tomato, sliced

1 cucumber, sliced

¼ cup extra-virgin olive oil

Salt

Freshly ground black pepper

Sliced fresh basil, for garnish (optional)

1. Preheat the oven to 275°F.

2. Cook the barley according to the package directions.

3. Wrap the flank steak and sweet potato in aluminum foil and warm in the oven for about 8 minutes.

4. Evenly distribute the cooked barley among 4 serving bowls. Top with the arugula, tomato, cucumber, sweet potato, and steak slices.

5. Drizzle 1 tablespoon of olive oil over each bowl and season with salt and pepper. Garnish with fresh basil (if using) and serve.

VARIATION TIP: Make your Buddha bowl spicy with a drizzle of sriracha. For a creamy addition, add a dollop of low-fat plain Greek yogurt. If you don't have barley on hand, use quinoa or rice.

PER SERVING: CALORIES: 527; FAT: 25G; SATURATED FAT: 3G; CHOLESTEROL: 45MG; CARBOHYDRATES: 45G; FIBER: 10G; PROTEIN: 31G; SODIUM: 669MG

CHICKEN, SPINACH & SWEET POTATO STEW, PAGE 143

CHAPTER SEVEN

Pressure Cooker and Slow Cooker Meals

PRESSURE COOKER

SLOW COOKER

Broccoli Egg Bites (Mini-Omelets)

MAKES 7 EGG BITES • PREP TIME: 15 MINUTES • COOK TIME: 20 MINUTES

If you have been using your pressure cooker for a while, you are probably familiar with some of the accessories you can purchase for it. Silicone pans and molds are perfect to use in a pressure cooker, and the egg bite mold is one of my favorites. If you don't have the mold, use small mason jars. Cover each one with aluminum foil and carefully stack them in your pressure cooker on the rack.

Nonstick cooking spray, for coating

¼ cup finely chopped broccoli

4 large eggs

⅔ cup shredded low-fat Cheddar cheese

½ cup cottage cheese

¼ cup half-and-half or coconut milk

1 teaspoon salt

¼ teaspoon freshly ground black pepper

1 cup water

Chopped fresh flat-leaf parsley or basil, for garnish

1. Coat a silicone egg bite mold with nonstick cooking spray.

2. Divide the broccoli among the prepared cups.

3. In a blender, combine the eggs, Cheddar cheese, cottage cheese, half-and-half, salt, and pepper. Process until smooth. Pour the egg mixture into the prepared mold, filling each cup about two-thirds full. Cover the mold with foil and crimp the sides around the mold to seal.

4. Pour the water into the pressure cooker and place the trivet into the pot.

5. Make a foil sling by folding a long piece of foil in half, or use a silicone sling. Place the sling under the mold and use it to lift the mold into the pot. Tuck in the foil sling if it extends beyond the top of the pot. Place the lid on the pressure cooker and seal it, making sure the pressure release valve is closed. Select Steam mode for 8 minutes.

6. When the cooking cycle is complete, let the pressure release naturally for 10 minutes, then quick-release any remaining pressure. Carefully open and remove the lid. Use the foil sling to remove the egg bites from the pot. Remove the foil cover and turn the mold over a plate to release the egg bites.

7. Sprinkle the egg bites with parsley.

VARIATION TIP: Place any fillings you like in the cups before pouring in the egg mixture. I like using 4 cooked and crumbled bacon slices. I also make these with pepperoni or cooked sausage and serve with a side of marinara for a pizza egg bite option. The kids love them.

PER SERVING (1 EGG BITE): CALORIES: 97; FAT: 6G; SATURATED FAT: 3G; CHOLESTEROL: 117MG; CARBOHYDRATES: 1G; FIBER: <1G; PROTEIN: 9G; SODIUM: 521MG

Chicken Gnocchi Soup

SERVES 4 • PREP TIME: 20 MINUTES • COOK TIME: 20 MINUTES

This recipe is a nod to one of my favorite restaurant soups. The pillowy soft gnocchi sets this soup apart from others. I use store-bought gnocchi, but you can make yours at home, if you like.

1 tablespoon extra-virgin olive oil

1½ pounds boneless, skinless chicken breast, cut into 1-inch chunks

½ cup chopped celery

½ cup chopped onion

3 cups low-sodium chicken broth

1 cup julienned carrots

½ teaspoon dried thyme

1 cup half and half

1 (1-pound) package shelf-stable gnocchi

2 cups fresh spinach

1. Select Sauté on your pressure cooker and heat the olive oil until hot.

2. Add the chicken, celery, and onion. Sauté for about 5 minutes, or until the chicken is browned and the vegetables are tender.

3. Stir in the chicken broth, carrots, and thyme, stirring until well combined. Place the lid on the pressure cooker and seal it, making sure the pressure release valve is closed. Select Manual and High Pressure for 4 minutes.

4. When the cooking cycle is complete, quick-release the pressure and carefully open and remove the lid.

5. Change the pressure cooker mode to Sauté and carefully stir in the half and half, gnocchi, and spinach. Bring the soup to a boil. Cook for about 3 minutes, or until the gnocchi are tender, stirring frequently.

VARIATION TIP: Look for cauliflower gnocchi at the store and substitute it for regular gnocchi for an extra dose of healthy vegetables.

PER SERVING: CALORIES: 501; FAT: 15G; SATURATED FAT: 6G; CHOLESTEROL: 159MG; CARBOHYDRATES: 45G; FIBER: 5G; PROTEIN: 46G; SODIUM: 567MG

Vegetable Beef Stew

SERVES 4 • PREP TIME: 15 MINUTES • COOK TIME: 25 MINUTES

This easy stew is as flavorful as one that has been cooking all day. Tender beef with tons of healthy vegetables–this is one soothing meal. Who ever said comfort food wasn't good for you?

1 tablespoon extra-virgin olive oil

1 pound beef stew meat

4 cups low-sodium beef broth

2 large Russet potatoes, peeled and cut into ½-inch dice

1 celery stalk, diced

1 (12-ounce) bag frozen mixed peas, carrots, corn, and green beans

1 teaspoon dried rosemary

1 teaspoon dried thyme

1 teaspoon salt

¼ teaspoon freshly ground black pepper

1. Select Sauté on the pressure cooker and heat the olive oil until hot.

2. Add the beef and sauté for about 3 minutes per side, or until browned on all sides.

3. Stir in the beef broth, potatoes, celery, mixed vegetables, rosemary, thyme, salt, and pepper, stirring until well combined.

4. Place the lid on the pressure cooker and seal shut, making sure the pressure release valve is closed. Select Manual and High Pressure for 10 minutes.

5. When the cooking cycle is complete, let the pressure release naturally for 10 minutes, then quick-release any remaining pressure. Carefully open and remove the lid.

COOKING TIP: To make this recipe in your slow cooker, place all the ingredients in the cooker. Cover the cooker and cook on low heat for 7 hours or on high heat for 4 hours.

PER SERVING: CALORIES: 412; FAT: 10G; SATURATED FAT: 3G; CHOLESTEROL: 75MG; CARBOHYDRATES: 47G; FIBER: 6G; PROTEIN: 35G; SODIUM: 1,147MG

Teriyaki Salmon with Green Beans

SERVES 4 • PREP TIME: 15 MINUTES, PLUS 30 MINUTES MARINATING
COOK TIME: 15 MINUTES

The pressure cooker does an amazing job of keeping food moist, making it ideal for cooking fish. The key is to make sure you allow at least 30 minutes to marinate the salmon before putting it into the pressure cooker.

½ cup low-sodium
    soy sauce

¼ cup honey

2 tablespoons sesame oil

6 garlic cloves, peeled

4 (6-ounce) skin-on
    salmon fillets

Salt

Freshly ground black
    pepper

1 cup water, plus
    1 tablespoon

1 pound green beans,
    washed and trimmed,
    or 1 (1-pound)
    package microwavable
    frozen green beans

1 teaspoon cornstarch

Scallions, for garnish
    (optional)

Sesame seeds, for garnish
    (optional)

1. In a small bowl, whisk the soy sauce, honey, sesame oil, and garlic until well combined. Pour half the marinade into a large bowl or gallon-size resealable bag, and reserve the remaining marinade for later.

2. Season the salmon fillets all over with salt and pepper and place them in the bag, turning the salmon to coat it in the marinade. Refrigerate for 30 minutes to marinate.

3. Pour 1 cup of water into the pressure cooker and place the trivet into the pot. Remove the salmon from the marinade and discard the used marinade. Place the salmon, skin-side down, on the rack. Place the lid on the pressure cooker and seal it, making sure the pressure release valve is closed. Select Steam mode for 4 minutes.

4. While the salmon cooks, steam the green beans to your desired doneness.

5. When the pressure cooking cycle is complete, quick-release the pressure. Carefully open and remove the lid.

6. Transfer the salmon to a serving plate and cover with aluminum foil to keep warm.

7. Discard the liquid left in the pressure cooker. Replace the pot and select Sauté. Add the reserved marinade and bring to a boil.

8. In a small dish, whisk the cornstarch and remaining 1 tablespoon of water until dissolved. Whisk the slurry into the boiling marinade and cook for 2 to 3 minutes, or until the sauce starts to thicken. Turn off the pressure cooker. Serve the sauce over the salmon with the green beans on the side. Garnish with scallions (if using) and sesame seeds (if using).

COOKING TIP: If your fillets will not fit on the rack, make individual foil packets and stack them on top of each other.

PER SERVING: CALORIES: 313; FAT: 11G; SATURATED FAT: 2G; CHOLESTEROL: 83MG; CARBOHYDRATES: 20G; FIBER: 4G; PROTEIN: 36G; SODIUM: 1,125MG

Vegetarian Stuffed Peppers

SERVES 4 • PREP TIME: 15 MINUTES • COOK TIME: 25 MINUTES

I love turning a classic recipe into something different—for instance, making these with mushrooms and not meat. This recipe includes cooked rice, so be sure you have some prepped (or use leftovers).

2 cups cooked white rice

1 (14.5-ounce) can diced Italian-seasoned tomatoes (or add 1 teaspoon Italian seasoning to a can of regular diced tomatoes)

2 (4-ounce) cans sliced mushrooms, drained and finely chopped

1 tablespoon low-sodium soy sauce

1 teaspoon garlic powder

Salt

Freshly ground black pepper

4 bell peppers, any color, tops, ribs, and seeds removed and discarded

1 cup water

1 cup shredded part-skim mozzarella cheese

1. In a large bowl, stir together the cooked rice, tomatoes, mushrooms, soy sauce, and garlic powder. Season with salt and black pepper and stir to combine. Fill each bell pepper with the rice mixture.

2. Pour the water into the pressure cooker and place the trivet into the pot. Place the peppers on the trivet. Place the lid on the pressure cooker and seal it, making sure the pressure release valve is closed. Select Manual and High Pressure for 3 minutes.

3. When the cooking cycle is complete, let the pressure release naturally for 5 minutes, then quick-release any remaining pressure. Carefully open and remove the lid. Let the steam dissipate, and then sprinkle the tops of each bell pepper with the mozzarella cheese. Place the lid back on the pot, but don't seal it. Let sit for about 2 minutes to allow the cheese to melt.

COOKING TIP: You can also make these peppers in the slow cooker or in the oven. For the slow cooker, assemble the peppers as directed and place them in the cooker on low heat for 6 to 7 hours or on high heat for 3 to 4 hours. Alternatively, bake at 350°F for about 1 hour, or until the peppers are tender but not mushy.

PER SERVING: CALORIES: 279; FAT: 5G; SATURATED FAT: 3G; CHOLESTEROL: 15MG; CARBOHYDRATES: 44G; FIBER: 5G; PROTEIN: 14G; SODIUM: 533MG

Chicken & Rice

SERVES 4 • PREP TIME: 15 MINUTES • COOK TIME: 40 MINUTES

This healthy version of chicken and rice includes brown rice, fresh mushrooms, and carrots, and it's easy to make in your pressure cooker. You can use any type of rice you like (see cooking tip to adjust the cooking time).

1 tablespoon extra-virgin olive oil

1 pound boneless, skinless chicken breasts

1 cup sliced mushrooms

1 cup julienned carrots

½ cup diced onion

3 garlic cloves, minced

1 teaspoon dried thyme

1 teaspoon salt

½ teaspoon freshly ground black pepper

2 cups low-sodium chicken broth

1 cup brown rice

1. Select Sauté on the pressure cooker and combine the olive oil and chicken in the pot. Sear the chicken for about 4 minutes per side. The chicken will not be cooked through.

2. Stir in the mushrooms, carrots, onion, garlic, thyme, salt, and pepper.

3. Add the chicken broth and rice to the pot and mix well. Place the lid on the pressure cooker and seal it, making sure the pressure release valve is closed. Select Manual and High Pressure for 20 minutes.

4. When the cooking cycle is complete, quick-release the pressure. Carefully open and remove the lid. Let the steam dissipate, then transfer the chicken to a bowl. Let it cool slightly before shredding it with 2 forks. Mix the chicken back into the rice and vegetables.

COOKING TIP: If you use white rice, cook at High Pressure for 10 minutes.

PER SERVING: CALORIES: 336; FAT: 8G; SATURATED FAT: 1G; CHOLESTEROL: 65MG; CARBOHYDRATES: 42G; FIBER: 4G; PROTEIN: 29G; SODIUM: 819MG

Chicken Burrito Bowls

SERVES 4 • PREP TIME: 15 MINUTES • COOK TIME: 30 MINUTES

I make this recipe at least once a week. My kids love it, my husband loves it, and I love it. The best part? It really is a dump-it-and-forget-it type of meal, the perfect recipe for a busy weeknight dinner.

1½ pounds boneless, skinless chicken breasts, cut into bite-size pieces

1 (15-ounce) can low-sodium black beans, rinsed and drained

1 cup frozen corn

2 cups low-sodium chicken broth

1 cup salsa

1 (1-ounce) packet taco seasoning

1 cup brown rice (see tip)

1 cup shredded low-fat Cheddar cheese (optional)

Low-fat plain Greek yogurt, for serving (optional)

1. Put the chicken in the electric pressure cooker pot. Cover it with the black beans, corn, chicken broth, and salsa.

2. Sprinkle the taco seasoning over the mixture and stir to combine.

3. Distribute the rice on top, pushing it down so the liquid covers it. Do not stir.

4. Place the lid on the pressure cooker and seal it, making sure the pressure release valve is closed. Select Manual and High Pressure for 20 minutes.

5. When the cooking cycle is complete, quick-release the pressure. Carefully open and remove the lid.

6. Stir the mixture, divide it into serving bowls, top each with ¼ cup of Cheddar cheese (if using), and a dollop of yogurt (if using).

PRESSURE COOKING TIP: If you would like to use white rice, decrease the broth to 1 cup and the cooking time to 10 minutes.

COOKING TIP: To make this in a slow cooker, combine the chicken, black beans, corn, chicken broth, salsa, and taco seasoning. Stir well. Cook on low heat for 4 to 5 hours. Cook the rice separately; stir it into the chicken before serving.

PER SERVING: CALORIES: 510; FAT: 6G; SATURATED FAT: 1G; CHOLESTEROL: 98MG; CARBOHYDRATES: 71G; FIBER: 9G; PROTEIN: 48G; SODIUM: 1,038MG

Cashew Chicken

SERVES 4 • PREP TIME: 15 MINUTES • COOK TIME: 25 MINUTES

This is one of the first meals I made in my pressure cooker, and it's still one of my favorites. I love cashews, and this recipe is so easy to make.

2 tablespoons extra-virgin olive oil

1 pound boneless, skinless chicken breasts, cut into 1-inch dice

3 garlic cloves, minced

½ cup low-sodium soy sauce

¼ cup water

1 tablespoon rice vinegar

1 tablespoon light brown sugar

1 tablespoon hoisin sauce

1 bell pepper, any color, chopped

1 cup unsalted roasted cashews

2 cups cooked white rice, warmed

2 scallions, thinly sliced (optional)

1. Select Sauté on the pressure cooker and heat the olive oil until hot.

2. Add the chicken and garlic. Sauté for about 4 minutes, stirring occasionally, or until the chicken is cooked through.

3. Stir in the soy sauce, water, vinegar, brown sugar, and hoisin sauce.

4. Stir in the bell pepper. Place the lid on the pressure cooker and seal it, making sure the pressure release valve is closed. Select Manual and High Pressure for 8 minutes.

5. When the cooking cycle is complete, quick-release the pressure. Carefully open and remove the lid.

6. Stir in the cashews and let sit for a few minutes to warm. Serve the cashew chicken over rice and garnish with the scallions (if using).

COOKING TIP: If you're concerned about sodium, reduce the hoisin sauce to 1½ teaspoons and increase the brown sugar by 1½ teaspoons. Reduce the soy sauce to ¼ cup and increase the water to ½ cup.

PER SERVING: CALORIES: 536; FAT: 26G; SATURATED FAT: 5G; CHOLESTEROL: 65MG; CARBOHYDRATES: 47G; FIBER: 2G; PROTEIN: 33G; SODIUM: 1,402MG

Chicken Cacciatore

SERVES 4 TO 6 • PREP TIME: 10 MINUTES • COOK TIME: 40 MINUTES

This traditional dish is ready in no time when cooked in a pressure cooker. This recipe calls for black olives, but you can use Kalamata olives instead.

3 teaspoons extra-virgin olive oil, divided

6 thin-cut chicken breasts

1 green bell pepper, diced

½ onion, diced

4 garlic cloves, minced

¼ cup water

¼ cup sliced black olives

1 (15-ounce) can crushed tomatoes

1 teaspoon dried oregano

1 teaspoon dried thyme

Salt

Freshly ground black pepper

2 tablespoons chopped fresh basil (optional)

1. Select Sauté on the pressure cooker and heat 1½ teaspoons of olive oil. Working in batches, cook the chicken for 2 minutes per side, turning, or until browned on both sides. Transfer to a medium bowl; repeat with the remaining olive oil.

2. Add the bell pepper and onion to the pot. Sauté for 4 to 5 minutes, stirring occasionally, or until the onion is translucent.

3. Add the garlic and cook for 30 seconds. Transfer the vegetables to the bowl with the chicken.

4. Add the water to pot, stirring to scrape up any browned bits. Turn off Sauté mode.

5. Return the chicken and vegetables to the pot. Stir in the olives, tomatoes, oregano, and thyme. Season with salt and black pepper. Place the lid on the pressure cooker and seal it, making sure the pressure release valve is closed. Select High Pressure for 3 minutes.

6. When the cooking cycle is complete, let the pressure release naturally for 5 minutes, then quick-release any remaining pressure. Carefully open and remove the lid. Select Sauté again and cook for about 10 minutes to thicken the sauce.

7. Spoon the sauce over the chicken, and garnish with basil (if using). Refrigerate leftovers in an airtight container for up to 4 days.

PER SERVING: CALORIES: 245; FAT: 9G; SATURATED FAT: 1G; CHOLESTEROL: 98MG; CARBOHYDRATES: 9G; FIBER: 2G; PROTEIN: 39G; SODIUM: 465MG

Cajun Sausage with Sweet Potatoes & Green Beans

SERVES 4 TO 6 • PREP TIME: 15 MINUTES • COOK TIME: 15 MINUTES

I read that a similar recipe is called Hoosier stew, which would be fitting because I currently reside in Indiana, the Hoosier state. This classic dish gets a spicy kick from the Cajun seasoning, which you can adjust to your preference.

2 large sweet potatoes, cut into ½-inch cubes

½ onion, chopped

8 ounces white button mushrooms, stemmed (optional)

1 pound green beans, trimmed

1 pound smoked turkey sausage, cut into ½-inch-thick rounds

1½ teaspoons Cajun seasoning

1 cup low-sodium chicken broth

Salt

Freshly ground black pepper

1. Place the sweet potatoes in the pressure cooker pot. Layer the onion, mushrooms (if using), green beans, and sausage on top. Sprinkle in the Cajun seasoning and pour the chicken broth over everything.

2. Place the lid on the pressure cooker and seal it, making sure the pressure release valve is closed. Select Manual and High Pressure for 4 minutes.

3. When the cooking cycle is complete, let the pressure release naturally for 10 minutes, then quick-release any remaining pressure. Carefully open and remove the lid. Taste and season with salt and pepper, as needed.

INGREDIENT TIP: I like using smoked turkey sausage because it is a little leaner than pork. You can use any type of smoked sausage you like. If you use a spicy variety, you might want to reduce the amount of Cajun seasoning.

PER SERVING: CALORIES: 325; FAT: 12G; SATURATED FAT: 4G; CHOLESTEROL: 60MG; CARBOHYDRATES: 36G; FIBER: 7G; PROTEIN: 21G; SODIUM: 1,468MG

Easy Beef & Broccoli

SERVES 4 • PREP TIME: 15 MINUTES • COOK TIME: 30 MINUTES

The brown sugar in the sauce provides a bit of sweetness, which is likely why it's a hit with kids. For adults, you can add a little heat, too: Try a dash of sriracha before serving. I love that sweet-and-spicy combination.

1 head broccoli, cut into florets

2 tablespoons extra-virgin olive oil

1 pound beef stew meat

½ cup chopped onion

3 garlic cloves, minced

½ teaspoon salt

½ teaspoon freshly ground black pepper

1 cup low-sodium beef broth

¼ cup low-sodium soy sauce

2 tablespoons light brown sugar or honey

2 cups cooked rice or couscous, warmed

Sesame seeds, for garnish (optional)

1. Place the broccoli in a large microwave-safe bowl. Microwave for about 6 minutes, or until tender. Set aside.

2. Select Sauté mode on the pressure cooker and heat the olive oil until hot.

3. Add the beef, onion, and garlic. Sauté for about 5 minutes, stirring occasionally, or until the beef is browned on all sides and the onion is translucent. Season with the salt and pepper.

4. Stir in the beef broth, soy sauce, and brown sugar. Place the lid on the pressure cooker and seal it, making sure the pressure release valve is closed. Select Manual and High Pressure for 10 minutes.

5. When the cooking cycle is complete, quick-release the pressure. Carefully open and remove the lid.

6. Using a slotted spoon, transfer the beef to a bowl. Select Sauté mode again and bring the sauce to a boil, stirring consistently. Cook for about 5 minutes, or until the mixture thickens.

7. Stir in the beef and add the broccoli. Serve over rice and garnish with sesame seeds (if using).

PER SERVING: CALORIES: 426; FAT: 14G; SATURATED FAT: 3G; CHOLESTEROL: 75MG; CARBOHYDRATES: 45G; FIBER: 5G; PROTEIN: 34G; SODIUM: 1,085MG

Apple Granola Oatmeal

SERVES 6 • PREP TIME: 10 MINUTES • COOK TIME: 5 TO 6 HOURS

This recipe works best with a programmable slow cooker so you can time it to greet you in the morning. No programmable slow cooker? No worries. Add this recipe to your Sunday meal prep rotation and breakfast for the week is solved. It reheats well in the microwave—simply add a dash of milk and heat it in 30-second increments until warm. Steel-cut oats have fewer calories than old-fashioned oats and contain more fiber.

2 cups unsweetened applesauce

2 apples, peeled, cored, and diced

½ cup raisins (optional)

⅓ cup honey

1½ teaspoons ground cinnamon

½ teaspoon salt

1½ cups steel-cut oats

3 cups almond milk

Chopped walnuts, for serving (optional)

1. In a slow cooker, stir together the applesauce, apples, raisins (if using), honey, cinnamon, salt, and oats.

2. Stir in the almond milk and mix well.

3. Cover the cooker and cook on low heat for 5 to 6 hours.

4. Serve topped with walnuts (if using). Refrigerate leftovers in an airtight container for up to 4 days.

COOKING TIP: I highly recommend using a slow cooker liner for this recipe. The oats tend to stick to the pot, and the liner makes cleanup a breeze.

PER SERVING: CALORIES: 286; FAT: 4G; SATURATED FAT: 1G; CHOLESTEROL: 0MG; CARBOHYDRATES: 62G; FIBER: 7G; PROTEIN: 7G; SODIUM: 271MG

White Chicken Chili

SERVES 6 • PREP TIME: 10 MINUTES • COOK TIME: 6 TO 8 HOURS

During winter months, this dish is one of my most requested meals. It is also great when entertaining a large group or for a potluck. The slow cooker is an easy way to transport it and keep it warm.

2 pounds boneless, skinless chicken thighs

2 teaspoons ground cumin

1 teaspoon garlic powder

1 teaspoon onion powder

1 (25-ounce) can hominy, rinsed and drained

1 (14-ounce) can white beans, rinsed and drained

1 cup frozen corn

1 (4-ounce) can diced green chiles

4 cups low-sodium chicken broth

Salt

Freshly ground black pepper

1. In a slow cooker, combine the chicken, cumin, garlic powder, onion powder, hominy, white beans, corn, green chiles, and chicken broth.

2. Cover the cooker and cook on low heat for 6 to 8 hours or on high heat for 4 to 6 hours.

3. Remove the chicken and place it on a cutting board. Let cool slightly, then dice or shred the chicken. Return the chicken to the slow cooker and stir to combine.

4. Taste and season with salt and pepper. Refrigerate leftovers in an airtight container for up to 4 days.

SUBSTITUTION TIP: If your family doesn't like hominy or you don't have it on hand, use more corn. The dish will have a slightly sweeter taste.

PER SERVING: CALORIES: 352; FAT: 11G; SATURATED FAT: 3G; CHOLESTEROL: 120MG; CARBOHYDRATES: 34G; FIBER: 7G; PROTEIN: 29G; SODIUM: 538MG

Chicken, Spinach & Sweet Potato Stew

SERVES 6 • PREP TIME: 10 MINUTES • COOK TIME: 7 TO 8 HOURS

This is a hearty chicken stew. I love that I can dump everything into the slow cooker in the morning and it is ready by dinnertime. I often throw in other ingredients I have on hand, such as diced bell pepper or leftover rice.

3 sweet potatoes, peeled and cut into 1-inch dice

1 pound bone-in chicken thighs

2 celery stalks, chopped

1 onion, chopped

2 (32-ounce) cartons low-sodium chicken broth

1 tablespoon Italian seasoning

2 teaspoons kosher salt

2 cups fresh spinach

1 tablespoon chopped fresh parsley

1. In a slow cooker, stir together the sweet potatoes, chicken, celery, and onion.

2. Add the chicken broth, Italian seasoning, and salt and stir to combine.

3. Cover the cooker and cook on low heat for 7 to 8 hours or on high heat for 4 to 6 hours.

4. With 1 hour of cooking time left, stir in the spinach.

5. Transfer the chicken to a cutting board and let cool slightly. Using 2 forks, shred the chicken and stir it back into the slow cooker. Serve garnished with the parsley. Refrigerate leftovers in an air-tight container for up to 4 days.

SUBSTITUTION TIP: Substitute another leafy vegetable for the spinach, such as kale, collard greens, or chard, based on your preference or what's in the refrigerator.

PER SERVING: CALORIES: 264; FAT: 12G; SATURATED FAT: 4G; CHOLESTEROL: 64MG; CARBOHYDRATES: 20G; FIBER: 3G; PROTEIN: 17G; SODIUM: 955MG

Butternut Squash Risotto

SERVES 4 • PREP TIME: 10 MINUTES • COOK TIME: 4 TO 6 HOURS (SEE TIP)

Risotto is so delicious, and this healthier version is a great everyday dish. Butternut squash provides fiber, potassium, and vitamin A in this recipe, minus the usual loads of cream and butter. Making risotto in a slow cooker is so much easier than on the stovetop–no constant stirring. I highly recommend it.

1¼ cups Arborio rice

2 tablespoons extra-virgin olive oil

4 cups low-sodium vegetable broth

1 small onion, chopped

2 garlic cloves, minced

2 tablespoons finely chopped fresh sage

1 teaspoon salt

¼ teaspoon freshly ground black pepper

1 (12-ounce) bag frozen butternut squash (no need to thaw)

¼ cup grated Parmesan cheese

1. In a slow cooker, stir together the rice and olive oil to coat the rice well.

2. Add the vegetable broth, onion, garlic, sage, salt, and pepper. Stir to combine.

3. Cover the cooker and cook on low heat for 4 to 6 hours. With 1 hour of cooking time left, add the squash (see tip).

4. Before serving, stir in the Parmesan cheese.

COOKING TIP: If you're away from the house for the whole day and need a longer cook time or cannot add ingredients during the cooking, assemble everything the night before or the morning of your meal prep day. Dump it in the slow cooker when you have 2 hours to spare, and cook, covered, on high heat for 2 hours.

VARIATION TIP: You can make any type of risotto with this recipe. Use pumpkin or acorn squash instead of butternut squash. With pumpkin, simply roast it, mash the flesh, and stir it in. Add some cinnamon; it changes the entire flavor profile.

PER SERVING: CALORIES: 354; FAT: 9G; SATURATED FAT: 2G; CHOLESTEROL: 5MG; CARBOHYDRATES: 58G; FIBER: 3G; PROTEIN: 8G; SODIUM: 839MG

Pineapple Pork Loin

SERVES 6 • PREP TIME: 15 MINUTES • COOK TIME: 8 HOURS

I love a good sweet-and-savory combination, and pineapple and pork deliver here. This recipe is also tasty with chicken. Replace the pork with chicken breasts and keep the cooking time the same. Serve with rice and steamed veggies, or as desired.

1 (3- to 4-pound) pork loin, trimmed

Salt

Freshly ground black pepper

2 tablespoons extra-virgin olive oil

¼ cup low-sodium soy sauce

⅓ cup honey

1 (23.5-ounce) can pineapple chunks in juice

8 garlic cloves, minced

1 tablespoon Dijon mustard

1. Season the pork loin all over with salt and pepper. Set aside.

2. In a skillet over medium-high, heat the olive oil until hot. Add the pork and sear each side for about 2 minutes, or until browned.

3. While the pork cooks, in a slow cooker, stir together the soy sauce, honey, and pineapple until well combined. In a small bowl, whisk the garlic and mustard.

4. Carefully brush the garlic-and-mustard sauce all over the browned pork loin and place the pork in the slow cooker.

5. Cover the cooker and cook on low heat for 8 hours.

VARIATION TIP: For a spicy kick, with the pineapple, add 1 jalapeño pepper, seeded and thinly sliced, or a few shakes of red pepper flakes.

PER SERVING: CALORIES: 643; FAT: 24G; SATURATED FAT: 6G; CHOLESTEROL: 179MG; CARBOHYDRATES: 37G; FIBER: 1G; PROTEIN: 68G; SODIUM: 571MG

Honey Garlic Chicken

If you are looking for an easy chicken dish the entire family will love, this recipe is for you. The savory sauce is delicious and has just the right amount of sweetness. With simple ingredients you probably have in your pantry, this is a great recipe you can make on busy nights.

½ cup honey

½ cup low-sodium soy sauce

¼ cup low-sodium chicken broth

2 tablespoons apple cider vinegar

3 garlic cloves, minced

4 bone-in chicken breasts or thighs, skin removed

1 pound baby red potatoes, halved

1 (1-pound) bag baby carrots

2 tablespoons fresh flat-leaf parsley (optional)

1. In a slow cooker, whisk the honey, soy sauce, chicken broth, vinegar, and garlic to blend.

2. Add the chicken breasts, potatoes, and carrots and stir to coat well.

3. Cover the cooker and cook on low heat for 8 hours or on high heat for 4 hours.

4. Serve garnished with the parsley (if using).

COOKING TIP: To make this in the pressure cooker: Whisk the honey, soy sauce, chicken broth, vinegar, and garlic in the pot to combine. Add the chicken, potatoes, and carrots and stir to coat. Place the lid on the pressure cooker and seal it, making sure the pressure release valve is closed. Select Manual and High Pressure for 10 minutes. When the cooking cycle is complete, quick-release the pressure. Carefully open and remove the lid.

PER SERVING: CALORIES: 418; FAT: 6G; SATURATED FAT: 2G; CHOLESTEROL: 80MG; CARBOHYDRATES: 66G; FIBER: 6G; PROTEIN: 28G; SODIUM: 1,356MG

Mediterranean Chicken

SERVES 4 TO 6 • PREP TIME: 5 MINUTES • COOK TIME: 6 TO 8 HOURS

Commercial Mediterranean spice blends can vary, but usually include a combination of coriander, cumin, cinnamon, nutmeg, salt, and pepper. It's a nice complement to chicken, lamb, or beef. This slow cooker Mediterranean-inspired meal combines chicken, tomatoes, and chickpeas to make a hearty meal that will warm you from the inside out.

4 bone-in chicken breasts, skin removed

2 pints grape tomatoes, halved

2 (15-ounce) cans low-sodium chickpeas, rinsed and drained

3 garlic cloves, minced

2 teaspoons extra-virgin olive oil

1 tablespoon freshly squeezed lemon juice

2 tablespoons Mediterranean spice blend (see tip)

1 teaspoon salt

1 lemon, sliced

Handful fresh cilantro (optional)

1. In a slow cooker, layer the chicken, tomatoes, chickpeas, and garlic.

2. Pour in the olive oil and lemon juice. Season with the Mediterranean spices and salt. Top with the lemon slices.

3. Cover the cooker and cook on low heat for 6 to 8 hours or on high heat for 4 hours. Top with cilantro (if using) and serve.

INGREDIENT TIP: Make your own Mediterranean spice mix: In a small bowl, whisk 3 tablespoons dried rosemary, 2 tablespoons ground cumin, 2 tablespoons ground coriander, 1 tablespoon dried oregano, 1½ teaspoons ground cinnamon, and 1 teaspoon salt. This makes about ⅓ cup of spice. Store in an airtight container.

PER SERVING: CALORIES: 419; FAT: 11G; SATURATED FAT: 2G; CHOLESTEROL: 80MG; CARBOHYDRATES: 51G; FIBER: 15G; PROTEIN: 34G; SODIUM: 602MG

Slow Cooker Pork Carnitas

SERVES 6 • PREP TIME: 10 MINUTES • COOK TIME: 8 TO 10 HOURS

This recipe is so much better for you than the carnitas served in a restaurant. The pork is not deep-fried, but I promise you won't notice. Crisp the pork edges under the broiler if you would like some crunch. Serve this in tacos, with rice and beans, or in a salad.

2 teaspoons salt

1½ teaspoons chili powder

1 teaspoon freshly ground black pepper

1 teaspoon dried oregano

½ teaspoon ground cumin

4 garlic cloves, minced

4 pounds boneless pork shoulder (pork butt)

1 onion, chopped

1 cup low-sodium chicken broth

¾ cup freshly squeezed orange juice

Cooked rice, beans, or tortillas, for serving

1. In a small dish, whisk the salt, chili powder, pepper, oregano, cumin, and garlic to combine. Rub the spice mixture into the pork. Transfer the pork to a slow cooker.

2. Place the onion on top of the pork. Pour the chicken broth and orange juice into the slow cooker.

3. Cover the cooker and cook on low heat for 8 to 10 hours or on high heat for 6 hours. When the pork is done, let cool briefly, and shred using 2 forks. If you like your carnitas crispy, spread the shredded meat (not the juices) on a sheet pan and broil for 5 to 10 minutes, or until the edges of the meat start to crisp. Return the pork to the cooker.

4. Serve as desired.

LOVE YOUR LEFTOVERS: Refrigerate leftovers in an airtight container for up to 1 week. I enjoy making nachos with leftover carnitas or putting carnitas on top of my salad during the week.

PER SERVING: CALORIES: 592; FAT: 44G; SATURATED FAT: 15G; CHOLESTEROL: 156MG; CARBOHYDRATES: 6G; FIBER: 1G; PROTEIN: 41G; SODIUM: 1,021MG

Slow Cooker Italian Beef

SERVES 4 TO 6 • PREP TIME: 10 MINUTES • COOK TIME: 8 TO 10 HOURS

This is the best slow cooker roast recipe I have ever made. The low heat makes the beef fall-apart tender, while the peperoncini give it just a slightly spicy flavor that won't overwhelm young palates.

1 (2-pound) boneless chuck roast, trimmed

½ teaspoon salt

1 teaspoon freshly ground black pepper

2 cups low-sodium beef broth (use 2½ cups if not using the wine)

½ cup red wine (optional)

2 tablespoons Worcestershire sauce

3 garlic cloves, minced

3 tablespoons Italian seasoning

1 bay leaf

4 or 5 whole peperoncini

1. Season the roast all over with the salt and pepper.

2. In a skillet over medium-high, sear the roast for about 4 minutes per side to brown.

3. While the roast cooks, in a medium bowl, whisk the beef broth, red wine (if using), Worcestershire sauce, garlic, and Italian seasoning to combine.

4. Transfer the roast to the slow cooker and pour the broth mixture over the roast. Top with the bay leaf and peperoncini.

5. Cover the cooker and cook on low heat for 8 to 10 hours or high heat for 4 to 5 hours.

6. Remove the peperoncini, cool slightly, and chop them, discarding the seeds and stems. Mix the chopped peperoncini into the beef. Using 2 large forks, shred the beef and stir to combine it with the sauce.

SERVING TIP: This Italian beef is great served over mashed cauliflower or potatoes, or use it to make sandwiches. If you like, thicken the sauce with a little cornstarch mixed with water. Stir the slurry into the sauce and boil until well combined and thickened.

PER SERVING: CALORIES: 419; FAT: 16G; SATURATED FAT: 5G; CHOLESTEROL: 160MG; CARBOHYDRATES: 4G; FIBER: 1G; PROTEIN: 61G; SODIUM: 907MG

Measurement Conversions

VOLUME EQUIVALENTS (LIQUID)

US STANDARD	US STANDARD (OUNCES)	METRIC (APPROXIMATE)
2 tablespoons	1 fl. oz.	30 mL
¼ cup	2 fl. oz.	60 mL
½ cup	4 fl. oz.	120 mL
1 cup	8 fl. oz.	240 mL
1½ cups	12 fl. oz.	355 mL
2 cups or 1 pint	16 fl. oz.	475 mL
4 cups or 1 quart	32 fl. oz.	1 L
1 gallon	128 fl. oz.	4 L

OVEN TEMPERATURES

FAHRENHEIT (F)	CELSIUS (C) (APPROXIMATE)
250°	120°
300°	150°
325°	165°
350°	180°
375°	190°
400°	200°
425°	220°
450°	230°

VOLUME EQUIVALENTS (DRY)

US STANDARD	METRIC (APPROXIMATE)
⅛ teaspoon	0.5 mL
¼ teaspoon	1 mL
½ teaspoon	2 mL
¾ teaspoon	4 mL
1 teaspoon	5 mL
1 tablespoon	15 mL
¼ cup	59 mL
⅓ cup	79 mL
½ cup	118 mL
⅔ cup	156 mL
¾ cup	177 mL
1 cup	235 mL
2 cups or 1 pint	475 mL
3 cups	700 mL
4 cups or 1 quart	1 L

WEIGHT EQUIVALENTS

US STANDARD	METRIC (APPROXIMATE)
½ ounce	15 g
1 ounce	30 g
2 ounces	60 g
4 ounces	115 g
8 ounces	225 g
12 ounces	340 g
16 ounces or 1 pound	455 g

Index

Acknowledgments

To my husband, Joe, who is my rock, my best friend, and my biggest supporter. There is no way I could have completed this project without your encouragement.

To Jonah and Caroline, my two amazing kids. Thank you for believing in me even when I don't believe in myself. You are my why, you are my inspiration—and I love you both more than you can imagine.

To my parents, Mike and Sharon. Thank you for teaching me what hard work looks like. Thank you for making recipes with me during our trip back to Idaho for the holidays. Thank you for sending me ideas while I was writing this book. I am so grateful to have such loving parents.

To my family, friends, and loyal followers at AMomsImpression.com. Thank you for your encouragement and support.

To my editor, Cecily. Thank you for being patient and understanding throughout this process. Thank you for focusing my thoughts and encouraging me along the way.

About the Author

KATHY HODSON was born and raised in the Pacific Northwest until she moved to Indiana, where she met her husband, started her family, and began her career as an elementary school teacher. When her son was born 11 years ago, she started a blog, AMomsImpression.com, documenting her parenting adventures and sharing family-friendly recipes and crafts.

Four years ago, she left her career as a teacher to focus full-time on her website. She loves being a mom, being a wife, traveling, visiting her family back home, and all things Disney! Although she loves creating healthy recipes for her family and website, she is a sucker for Jelly Belly candies.

CPSIA information can be obtained
at www.ICGtesting.com
Printed in the USA
BVHW092212140520
579445BV00007B/34